THE SWEET DREAMS LOVE BOOK

Has this ever happened to you? You're at a party, a dance, or a basketball game. All of a sudden it happens—you meet someone, and *zap*! It's love at first sight. Or is it? Love at first sight is absolutely wonderful. It's magical and mysterious. It's also a fantasy.

If people could recognize true love at first glance, life (and love) would be a lot less complicated. But love is not always what it appears to be. That's why it should be looked at very closely—and that means looking beneath the surface.

Bantam Sweet Dreams Romances
Ask your bookseller for the books you have missed

Don't miss these special Sweet Dreams books

A Sweet Dreams Special

The
Sweet Dreams
Love Book

Understanding Your Feelings

Deidre S. Laiken and
Alan J. Schneider

BANTAM BOOKS
TORONTO · NEW YORK · LONDON · SYDNEY

RL 5, IL age 11 and up

THE SWEET DREAMS LOVE BOOK

A Bantam Book / February 1983

Sweet Dreams and its associated logo are registered trademarks of Bantam Books, Inc.
Registered in U.S. Patent and Trademark Office and elsewhere.

Cover photo by Pat Hill

ISBN 0-553-23288-6

Published simultaneously in the United States and Canada

Bantam Books are published by Bantam Books, Inc. Its trademark, consisting of the words ''Bantam Books'' and the portrayal of a rooster, is Registered in U.S. Patent and Trademark Office and in other countries. Marca Registrada. Bantam Books, Inc., 666 Fifth Avenue, New York, New York 10103.

PRINTED IN THE UNITED STATES OF AMERICA

O   0 9 8 7 6 5 4 3 2 1

This book is dedicated to
Berenice Hoffman—
who went the distance

Contents

Foreword

*L*ove is an important part of everyone's life. It's important when we're young and important as we grow older. Love nurtures and inspires us. But there is a lot to learn about love. The more you know about this emotion, the more likely it is that your experiences with it will be rewarding ones.

The Sweet Dreams Love Book talks about topics we all want to know more about. It discusses why we're attracted to certain people, why some of us seem to be afraid of love, and why others of us seem to fall headlong into "love traps." But more important, *The Sweet Dreams Love Book* gives practical advice that you can use to counteract jealousy, confusion, and even a broken heart. The authors show you how problems can be dealt with and solutions found.

The habits we develop as young people usually stay with us as we mature. Learning how to listen to someone else, how to consider another person's feelings, and how to make significant decisions about your own needs are important lessons you'll never forget. But these lessons are not taught in school. They are lessons you can learn only from experience. When you have questions, doubts, and uncertainties about love, *The Sweet Dreams Love Book* can help you. It may not have all the answers, but it does have information that can make the questions seem less formidable.

—ROBERT LLOYD GOLDSTEIN, M.D.
Diplomate of the American
Board of Psychiatry and Neurology
New York, N.Y.

Introduction

Q. What is love?

A. It's something that just *happens!*

Q. How will I know when I'm in love?

A. You'll just *know!*

Q. When will it happen to me?

A. When you grow up.

Q. But maybe I'm in love right now?

A. Don't be silly, you're too young. That's just puppy love.

Q. What's the difference between puppy love and real love?

A. Love can't be explained; you just have to *feel* it.

Does this conversation sound familiar? If you've ever wondered about love (who hasn't?), and if you've talked to an adult about it, you've probably gotten answers just like these. Most of the time people act as if love were something magical that must be felt, cannot be explained, and is *strictly for grown-ups.*

Love isn't magic, although it may feel that way sometimes. It's very real. It *can* be described, and it can be experienced by everyone, *regardless of age.* Understanding the process of love and learning how to make your love relationship work is what this book is all about.

Love is not simple. It involves emotions, and though emotions can be wonderful, they can also be confusing, confounding, and catastrophic. That's why you won't find any cute one-liners or catchy romantic phrases in this book. What you will find is information you can understand and suggestions you can apply to *your* life and *your* love relationships.

Learning about love means taking a good look at one of the main components of a love relationship—yourself. What are your fantasies, expectations, and hopes about love? Where do they come from? Do you think they'll ever come true, and can they last—forever? By the time you finish this book, you should not only know more about what love is—you should know more about who *you* are.

CHAPTER ONE

Someday Your Prince Will Come

*I*f you're like most people, you grew up hearing stories about Prince Charming and other perfect young men like him—tales of eternal, everlasting love. You listen to songs, watch movies, and read books about love. It seems as if everyone, everywhere, is thinking about just one thing. Thousands of times you've envisioned your "ideal mate," the person who will change your life and make you happy forever. You may even know how this special someone will look, talk, and behave. Maybe your ideal is someone specific; maybe he's even someone you see in everyday life. But then, he might be someone totally out of reach—a movie star, your math

1

teacher, or that person who doesn't even know you're alive.

Have you ever wondered how you developed this image of the "ideal mate?" Well, if you have, then you've taken the first step toward learning about the nature of love.

HOW ATTRACTIONS
ARE FORMED

At first glance, it may seem that nearly everyone you know is the same—they all dress alike, talk alike, even dance alike. But, inside, everyone is very different. Everyone has different expectations, fantasies, and ideas about love and the type of person he or she is likely to fall in love with. Some people, for example, picture falling in love in an exotic place, and imagine a whirlwind courtship and a romantic wedding. Other people have completely different ideas. One girl might plan to know the person she falls in love with for a long time, and fantasize about a lengthy relationship that might or might not include marriage. Another girl might never think that far ahead. Some people picture their ideal loves in complete detail, right down to color of hair and eyes; others have only vague ideas. The point is that your ideal love is someone you've thought about, imagined, and dreamed of for quite a while. The type of person you find attractive tells a lot about who *you* are and about what sorts of things *you* want and need.

Many diverse elements are involved in attraction, and that makes love a bit more complicated than a chance meeting with a tall dark stranger or a magical glance across a crowded room. Someday you may just meet a tall dark stranger, but if your fantasy is about a short blond guy, then it won't be the encounter you'd hoped for.

Why are certain people attracted to specific types? Why do you always seem to fall for blonds—or brunettes or redheads? How come you think that boys who wear glasses are terrific, while your best friend feels just the opposite? Why do you think a sense of humor or athletic ability is important in someone you're going to date, while some of your friends think that intellect and looks are the essential attributes? Once you know something about how attractions are formed, you won't need a fortune teller to predict who you'll be drawn to.

A LOOK AT THREE
"IDEAL MATES"

Three friends, Mark, Donna, and Jarrad, said this when they were asked to describe the type of person they'd be most likely to fall in love with:

MARK: When I think of love I see before me a gorgeous girl. She's tall and thin and has soft long red hair. She has a turned-up nose and a great dimple in her cheek that only shows when she laughs. She's very sexy, and she's crazy about me. Pleasing me is her number-one priority. She probably wants to get serious—become engaged and eventually get married. But I'm still young and have a lot of living to do, even though I love being with her. Eventually, I guess we *will* settle down and have a family.

DONNA: To me, love means being with someone I have a lot in common with. Sometimes when I'm alone, I think about my future husband. You know, I wonder where he is and what he's doing. I know exactly what he'll be like. He'll probably be a professional of some sort—a doctor or a lawyer. He'll be extremely intelligent and a good provider. I don't expect him to be rich, but he will make enough money so that we can live comfortably. I don't care much about the way he looks, as long as he's fairly attractive. But I do know that he will be very loyal to me, and gentle and kind. That's more important to me than looks.

JARRAD: When I think of falling in love, I think of a girl who's very exciting. Someone who is creative and in the arts. She could be an actress, a musician, or a painter. All I know is that she'll have an absorbing, creative career. She'll also love to travel and try new things.

She'll be the type of person who's always interested in growing and changing. She won't be a stay-at-home type, afraid to try new ideas and visit different places. Together we'll live this great life. We'll work on creative projects together, move around a lot, and never get bored. Our life will center around our work and our relationship with each other.

EVERYONE'S
• DIFFERENT

Mark, Donna, and Jarrad have three different images of the type of person they'd be most likely to fall in love with. Although they all go to the same school and are good friends, their descriptions of their ideal mates don't sound at all alike. Which answers did you find yourself agreeing with? Do you think that Mark's idea of a beautiful girl who is completely devoted to him is what love is all about? Maybe you agree with Donna's concept of love as a secure, comfortable relationship. Perhaps you are like Jarrad and desire someone with whom you can share interests and creativity. Maybe you agree a little with Mark, a little with Donna, and a little with Jarrad.

On the other hand, maybe *none* of these ideal mates appeals to you. The point is that everyone thinks of love in a different way. If you were to ask ten different people about their ideal loves, you'd get ten different answers. But each answer would give you important information— it would tell you a great deal about the person you had asked. By getting to know Mark, Donna, and Jarrad a little better, you can learn why they are attracted to the types of people they have described.

ATTRACTION IS WHAT YOU BRING TO IT

Mark comes from a family that places a very high value on physical beauty. Mark's mother has red hair and was a beauty contest winner before she married Mark's father, who was a star basketball player on his college team. Mark has many memories of conversations with his father in which he was told: "There are plenty of fish in the sea. Love is serious business. You're a good-looking boy, you come from a good-looking family. You'll be a lot happier if you pick a beautiful woman. You're handsome enough to pick and choose who you want. You'll always have the ladies chasing you, so pick a beauty."

Much of what Mark's dad has told him has already come true. Mark is a star football player, and all the girls are crazy about him. Mark always chooses the most beautiful girl. He figures if he just keeps doing this, he'll wind up pretty much like his dad—married to a redheaded beauty queen.

Donna's parents were divorced when she was three years old. She's an only child, and she spends a great deal of time alone because her mother works two jobs to support them. Donna remembers very little about her father. She knows he was a bartender when he married her mom. Her mother has also told her that he was unreliable and an alcoholic. Donna has felt very alone and insecure for most of her life. She has thought about her situation and about her parents' marriage. She has made up her mind that she will not end up like her mother—divorced and working two jobs. She has made a secret promise to herself that she will have a better life—a more secure and less lonely one. Security is the key to love for Donna; she wants a man who will be very different from her father. Her ideal man will be responsible, reliable, loyal, and a good provider.

Jarrad's parents own a small grocery store. They have worked seven days a week for as long as he can remember. They never complain about the work, but they have always said, "We wish we could have more time to enjoy the good things in life, like art and music." Although they cannot take the time to appreciate these things themselves, they have encouraged Jarrad to. He takes private piano lessons and has studied guitar and saxophone on his own. He plans a career in music.

Some of Jarrad's happiest times have been spent helping his parents out in the store. He realizes that his parents share a very special partnership—they may work hard all week, but they spend the time together. When Jarrad thinks of love, he thinks of someone who will share his creative interests and who will want to experience new and exciting life-styles. But that alone will not be enough. Since Jarrad has always admired the way his parents work together, he wants that kind of partnership for himself when he falls in love, and it's something his ideal mate will have to want, too.

LOVE =
SELF + SELF

Mark, Donna, and Jarrad are going to have three entirely different love experiences. They are individuals with distinctly separate backgrounds, attitudes, and values. But, most important, they have different *selves*.

Love is a relationship between two selves—your self and someone else's self. Your self is the sum total of all the different parts of your personality. It's your intellect, your emotions, and your sexuality. It is also all the things you carry around with you that you're not aware of—the unconscious things, like your memories, fears, fantasies, expectations, needs, values, prejudices—your entire background. Your self is a lot like your fingerprint—it both identifies you and makes you different from everyone else.

Your self grows and changes as you grow and change. It is the most wonderful and exciting thing about you. It's what you bring to a love relationship, and what you share with the person you love. But how can you be sure that you'll find someone else who appreciates the real you—the self you may be hiding from everyone you know?

MAKING THE
PIECES FIT

For centuries people have said that "love is a puzzle." Unfortunately, this statement alone won't help you to understand what love is all about. But if you look a little deeper, you'll find that there is some truth to the old saying. Think of love as a puzzle that is put together properly. The pieces of the puzzle are all the different aspects of your self plus someone else's self. When the pieces fit—when your intellect, your emotions, and your sexuality are in harmony with someone else's—you experience that "together feeling"—love.

Let's go back to Mark, Donna, and Jarrad and see how the love puzzle might work for them. All three have told us a lot about themselves. . . .

Part of Mark's self dreams of a gorgeous girl who will be devoted to him. In order for Mark to have a successful love relationship, he's going to have to find a girl who will have a complementary fantasy. In other words, he needs to find a girl he thinks is beautiful, and who has a dream of devoting herself to a boy like Mark.

Within Donna's self there are very strong feelings of insecurity. In order for her to have a successful love relationship, she'll need to find a boy whose inner feelings fit with hers—someone who wants to make a girl feel secure, protected, and safe.

Jarrad's self believes in creativity and partnership. To have a successful love relationship, he will need to find a girl who shares his creative talents *and* his desire to work as a team toward common goals.

Maybe Mark, Donna, and Jarrad won't find their ideals, but it's safe to predict the people they fall in love with will fit them in certain ways. And if the pieces fit badly, they will be in for rocky times. That's because, when love goes wrong, it's usually because the people involved haven't taken the time and effort to learn about themselves—or because they don't understand the self in someone else.

CHAPTER TWO

Love at First Sight

*H*as this ever happened to you? You're at a party, a dance, or a basketball game. All of a sudden it happens—you meet someone, and *zap!* It's love at first sight. Or is it? Love at first sight is absolutely wonderful. It's magical and mysterious. It's also a fantasy.

*FANTASY:
MEDICINE FOR
THE SELF*

All of us carry around hundreds of fantasies in our heads. We create them to make ourselves

11

feel good. Some fantasies keep us company when we are feeling lonely. Others act as a kind of dress rehearsal—they prepare us for experiences we may not have had yet. There are times in everyone's life when problems are very complicated. Often it's helpful to use fantasies to explore the many different solutions that exist, and then to pick out the best one and apply it to reality. Your fantasies are a natural and very healthy part of your self.

Some fantasies are entertaining and funny. Others are frightening. Have you ever had a scary fantasy, or a too-sexy one? Sometimes you might feel embarrassed by your fantasies. You might think that some of them are just plain stupid. But, like your dreams, your fantasies have meaning. If you can learn to listen to them, you will have the key to some important truths about yourself.

You create fantasies to help yourself deal with a problem, or to teach yourself more about who you really are. However, it's not always clear just how a particular fantasy is supposed to help you. If you misunderstand your fantasies, or ignore them completely, you can complicate your problems instead of easing them.

Some fantasies are obviously "out of this world," while others seem extremely real. And that can be confusing. Not too long ago, Ken had that kind of confusing experience. He was sure he had fallen in love at first sight. . . .

GETTING ZAPPED
BY LOVE

Ken was sitting in English class, and all of a sudden it happened. *Zap!* He was in love with Ronnie. The first sensation he was aware of was a strange and powerful feeling; it was like nothing he had ever experienced before. His heart was beating quickly. His hands began to sweat. He felt light-headed. He could see only one person in the whole world—Ronnie. There at the front of the English class was the perfect girl. As Ken sat there, he began to think:

"Ronnie, I love you. You are the most beautiful girl I have ever seen. You are the greatest, most wonderful human being in the entire world. It makes me feel fantastic just to sit here and look at you. Any boy would be thrilled, exalted, to have a single date with you. But who am I kidding? You'd never be interested in a guy like me. I'm not even popular. You probably get asked out ten times a week. You probably don't even go out with high school guys—just college men. If only I were taller, more of an athlete, or had a better sense of humor. Oh, what's the use? You'd probably only laugh at me if I ever got up the nerve to ask you out."

MAKING THE FIRST
MOVE

It's not quite clear how Ken could have such strong feelings for Ronnie, since he didn't really know her. But Ken was sure that this was the real thing; he was sure he had fallen hopelessly in love—at first sight. The problem was, how could he make Ronnie aware of his feelings? He tried to overcome his fear of asking her out by practicing in front of a mirror. But whenever he did that, he wound up thinking, "What's wrong with me? I'm no man. No girl would be interested in me. I'm a dud. A failure at sixteen."

Finally, Ken became so unhappy that he forced himself to call Ronnie. He figured he really had nothing to lose (except his unhappiness). To his surprise, she accepted a date with him. She even knew who he was! As soon as Ken hung up the telephone, his mind began to race:

"I can't believe she said yes! I feel sick. What will I talk about all night? I don't even have any decent clothes to wear. And where in the world can I take her? She's probably been to all the really good places in town. I don't want her to think that I haven't been around. I just hope I can pull this night off. I hope she won't find out what a loser I really am!"

REALITY . . . THE
BIG LETDOWN

When the big night finally rolled around, Ken managed to muster up all his courage, and he arrived at Ronnie's house right on time. They went to a movie and had a pizza afterwards. At the end of the evening, Ronnie told Ken that she'd had a wonderful time and hoped they would get together again soon.

You'd think that Ken would have felt wonderful about the way things had turned out. Surprisingly, he didn't feel that way at all. Instead, he felt disappointed and a little depressed. As he tried to go to sleep, Ken thought:

"That was a whole lot of worry for nothing. Ronnie is really nothing like I thought she would be. At first I was so nervous, I was practically shaking. The movie gave me a chance to calm down. By the time we got to the pizza place I was feeling pretty relaxed. That's when I realized that I had made a big mistake about Ronnie. She's not a woman of the world. Once we started talking, I saw that Ronnie really doesn't go out very much, and certainly not with college men. I'm probably one of the few guys she's ever dated. No wonder she jumped at the chance when I called her! Ronnie is really like most of the other girls at school. She's nice and she's cute, but she's just an immature kid. What I need is a woman of the world. Someone who has really been around. Someone who is different and exciting. What a disappointment! I feel down. When will it happen to me? When will I really fall in love?"

LOVING THE MOVIE, NOT THE SCREEN

Finding out who you are in love with takes time. No matter how badly you want to fall in love, you can't rush it. Many people believe that it's possible to fall in love at first sight. In fact, they're sure of it. Ken certainly was. But the truth is, Ken was "in love" with Ronnie long before he ever laid eyes on her. Before they even talked, he *thought* he knew all about her.

In his mind, Ken had an image of the girl he would fall in love with—the person he had been waiting for all his life. Suddenly he was sure Ronnie was that girl. But Ken was never in love with the real Ronnie. He was in love with his own fantasy, and he convinced himself that by going out with Ronnie, he could make all his dreams come true. In other words, Ken was not in love with a real person. For Ken, Ronnie was like a blank movie screen.

When you go to the movies, you're confronted by a blank screen. Then the lights go out, the camera is turned on, and, as if by magic, the blank screen is transformed. At the end of the movie you're left with many feelings, sensations, and thoughts. But, of course, your thoughts and feelings aren't about the movie screen itself. They are about *the images that were projected onto the screen.*

Now, Ken projected his images onto Ronnie—the images of his "dream girl," the girl he could fall in love with. He might just as easily have "fallen in love" with any other girl in his English class, because what he saw in Ronnie was just a reflection of his own fantasy. That fantasy had very little to do with Ronnie's real self. So-called "love at first sight" often works this way.

SEPARATING THE
IMAGE FROM
THE REALITY

How can you know when what you're feeling is genuine, and when you are just projecting your feelings onto someone else? If you take the time to separate the image from the reality, the movie from the screen, you will be less likely to wind up like Ken—disappointed and depressed. Let's go back to Ken's fantasy about Ronnie and see if we can turn the key and unlock the mystery of his "love at first sight."

MIRROR, MIRROR, ON THE WALL

Remember that fantasy is medicine for the self. What medicine could Ken have been looking for when he first created his wonderful "dream girl" fantasy?

To begin with, Ken imagined a girl who was not only beautiful, but sophisticated as well—a girl who was perfect. Now, if Ken were able to live out his fantasy and actually win over the perfect girl, he would feel pretty wonderful about himself. If someone perfect fell in love with Ken, it would mean that he was perfect, too.

When Ken discovered that Ronnie was not perfect, not his dream girl, he lost all interest in her. She became just like everybody else. Her imperfections turned Ken off. Why? Maybe because Ken had trouble accepting his *own* imperfections.

Remember when Ken stared into the mirror and called himself a "dud" and a "failure"? He was unable to accept the fact that he couldn't ask Ronnie out quickly and easily. He didn't think he was popular enough, tall enough, athletic enough, or funny enough. He was ashamed of his limitations. He put himself down. If he'd been able to, he would have run away from what he was. But, of course, he couldn't do that. By attempting to fall in love with Ronnie, he tried to create a relationship that would make him feel good about himself—a relationship that would make him feel perfect, in fact. And it just didn't work.

Everyone has limitations. Some people think they're too short, too tall, too fat, or too thin. It's just not possible to feel good about yourself *all* the time. There are times when you'll feel just like Ken—you'll look into the mirror and see only your limitations. Then you might become angry at yourself, judge yourself, even put yourself down. This can be painful and depressing. You begin to feel unhappy. You're just not good-looking enough, smart enough, or athletic enough. Then you begin to wish that you were all the things you're not. . . .

If these feelings start to take over, you may even forget about the good qualities you *do* have. Like Ken, you might think of yourself as a "dud" and a "failure." Then, instead of trying to improve and accept yourself, you will probably begin to fantasize. You will wish something magical would happen. You will wish that you could love and be loved by someone who has all the qualities you lack. When this happens, you're liable to find yourself falling in love "at first sight."

WHERE LOVE
REALLY BEGINS

The love-at-first-sight fantasy is one that usually doesn't come true. This is because *no one* outside yourself can make you feel good about being you. Love begins when you have learned to listen to, accept, and like yourself. Good feelings are catching. When you value who you are, then someone else can, too. But it must start with *you*, and not with somebody else. If you don't really like or accept yourself, you'll find it hard to believe that someone else might like or accept you. In fact, if someone did try to love you, you'd probably think there was something wrong with *him*. You might find yourself thinking, "What sort of a person could fall in love with a loser like me?"

The truth is, love *can* make you feel wonderful. But if you want the feeling to last, you need to know what real love is (and isn't), and how to make it work for you.

CHAPTER THREE

The Look of Love

Just think of all the expressions which imply that love has something to do with looking: "the look of love," "the eyes of love," "love at first sight." If people could recognize true love at first glance, life (and love) would be a lot less complicated. But love is not always what it appears to be. That's why it should be looked at very closely—and that means looking beneath the surface. What you see on the surface can be physical attraction, friendship, even infatuation—but is it love? Many people can't make that decision until it's too late. Then you're likely to hear the following:

"It wasn't really love—it was just an infatuation."

"I was sure it was love. But I got bored and broke it off."

"It was love, but he kept hurting me. Well, you know what they say: 'you always hurt the one you love.' "

"It was great at the beginning, but he turned out to be so immature. I guess it was just puppy love."

"We were very serious, but we outgrew each other."

"I'm really not surprised that it didn't work out. What can a person like me really expect?"

"I loved him, but he couldn't accept me for who I really am."

DIFFERENT STROKES WITH DIFFERENT FOLKS

Love is difficult to "see" because it has so many components. All your relationships bring out different parts of your self. If you're like most people, you probably enjoy different activities with different friends. You may love playing tennis with one friend, while you share your musical interest with another. There may be someone special with whom you enjoy discussing your feelings, fantasies, and ideas about life.

One friend may bring out your athletic side, another your creative side, and a third your emotional and intellectual sides. And if you're really lucky, you have a best friend, someone who brings out *many* aspects of your self, and with whom you can share many different activities. Being in love is like having a best friend—only it's better. It's more fun, exciting, and satisfying. That's because you share a lot more of your self when you're in love.

DON'T RUSH IT

Love takes time. It may seem that falling in love happens all at once, but that's only an illusion. It takes quite a while for you to discover and develop the many different parts of your self. Then you have to find someone whose personality and self will complement and harmonize with yours. And once you have found someone like that, someone who is capable of giving you what you need, you have to wait for love to develop.

Falling in love is the process of learning about another person, accepting him, and coming to like (not just love) him. This process may begin with a sudden physical attraction, but it takes much more than physical attraction to create lasting love.

LOVE HUNGER

Being patient is not always the easiest thing in the world. Waiting for all the conditions for love to be just right can be frustrating. First, you have to feel mature—and when does that happen? Then, you have to wait until you meet someone you can love. Now there's a *real* unknown—the waiting for *that* can seem to go on forever! Then you have to wait for love to grow. How long does that take? Sometimes it seems as if you have been waiting your whole life. And the more you wait, the more it seems as if everyone else in the world is in love and that it will never happen to you.

You might have noticed that you have been feeling this way most of the time, and that no matter what you do, you just can't shake the feeling. Don't panic! And don't hide your head in shame. What you're feeling is normal. It's called "love hunger," and it happens to everyone at one time or another.

Love hunger is usually activated by experiences and longings in your everyday life. Let's say, for example, that you have one of those horrible weeks when everything goes wrong. Probably you wind up feeling depressed and out of sorts. Before you know it, you find yourself wishing, even praying, for someone special to come along and take the pain away. You long for someone to make you feel better. In no time at all, you have a case of love hunger.

You might have had love hunger when you moved to a new neighborhood and didn't know a soul. At first you felt lonely and missed your old friends. Maybe you started to imagine that you'd never make another friend as long as you lived. Finally, you began to fantasize about someone special, someone who would make you feel terrific and wanted—someone who would love you.

You don't have to experience trauma (a horrible week, a move to a new neighborhood) to develop love hunger. How many times have you walked out of a movie and said to yourself, "I wish that I could meet someone like so-and-so—then all my problems would surely be over"? Did you know that you were experiencing love hunger?

RECOGNIZING YOUR OWN LOVE HUNGER

Television, radio, movies, and magazines all sell their products and services by stimulating your love hunger. The media work very hard to create the illusion that love is the answer to all of life's problems. They want to convince you that if you will just buy a particular product, go to a certain movie, or subscribe to a special magazine, you, too, will fall in love. These techniques usually work. That's because everyone wants to fall in love!

All sorts of situations feed love hunger. You can probably think of several events in your own life that stimulated feelings of love hunger. Sometimes a death, your parents' divorce, illness, or loneliness can cause intense emotional pain. This pain increases love hunger.

Understanding and recognizing love hunger is very important. That's because love hunger can cause you to do things that you wouldn't ordinarily do—like make mistakes about love. Love hunger can push you into a relationship that isn't good for you. It can make you believe that you have fallen in love, when what you have really fallen into is a love *trap!*

CHAPTER FOUR

Love Traps

Like most traps, a love trap is confining, uncomfortable, and difficult to escape. But a love trap is something you create yourself. When love hunger becomes intense and you don't really recognize it for what it is, you're likely to become involved in a relationship that is destructive, unfulfilling, or just plain dull. But you're trapped, because you've convinced yourself that this is "the real thing."

There are many different love traps. In this chapter you'll read about the more common ones. And maybe, just maybe, in the pages that follow, you'll read about someone you know.

Marsha loved Bruce. At least she *thought* she did. She did everything for him. Wherever Bruce went, she went. Whatever Bruce did, she did. They shared everything. They liked the same foods and the same music. They even had the same friends. Everyone noticed how close they were and jokingly called them the "Siamese twins."

Then one day, Bruce sat Marsha down and said he wasn't happy with the way things were going. He explained that he felt smothered, felt that she had taken away his individuality. Bruce told Marsha he wanted to break up. Marsha was devastated. She couldn't understand why Bruce was so unhappy, especially when *she* felt that things were so perfect. In Marsha's mind, she and Bruce were getting closer and falling more in love every day. She'd even been planning on getting engaged in a few years. Marsha was convinced that she and Bruce were made for each other.

THE TRAP: Marsha fell into a common love trap—she became a clinging vine. Her love hunger trapped her into a relationship that, in the end, self-destructed. Marsha wanted Bruce to be everything to her. She wanted to be close to him all the time. He was her whole life, and she only felt happy when she was with him. Whenever she was apart from him, she felt insecure; she wondered where he was and what he was doing. She imagined that when they weren't together, Bruce was with other girls. She got to be so anxious that, to relieve the anxiety, she would call Bruce on the phone. In long conversations Marsha would question Bruce about every detail of the time they had spent apart. And she always ended the conversation by trying to convince him to come to her house or to make a date for the following day.

Marsha managed to cling to Bruce in every way. She tried to eliminate anything that made him different from her. She figured that if they enjoyed all the same things, they could always do everything together. But, in the end, Marsha wrapped herself so tightly around Bruce that he had to stop seeing her in order to avoid being strangled.

How did all this come to happen? The answer lies in Marsha's insecurity. Her fear that she would lose Bruce made her cling too tightly—and the more afraid she became, the more tightly she clung. Finally she was clinging so tightly that what she feared most actually happened—Bruce broke up with her. He might have loved Marsha at one time, but, as he told her, he felt he was being smothered and just had to get away.

THE PLACATER

Bruce wasn't entirely free from blame in his relationship with Marsha. In his own way, he encouraged her and contributed to their break-up. Bruce fell into another kind of love trap. He became a placater—a person who simply can't say no. Bruce really didn't want to go along with a lot of what Marsha wanted. But Bruce's philosophy was, "Don't rock the boat unless it's absolutely necessary." Bruce never wanted to argue or disagree with Marsha, so he went along with her, never complaining about all the phone calls or all the togetherness. And, what's worse, Bruce never discussed his true feelings with Marsha. He held everything inside until he finally burst. All because he wanted to avoid unpleasantness. But, of course, Bruce couldn't avoid the weeks and months of dissatisfaction, and finally he had to face the most unpleasant fact of all—that he wanted to free himself from his relationship with Marsha.

THE TRAP: Placaters are not just people who are afraid to say no. They are people who are afraid to say what they feel, afraid to assert themselves, and, ultimately, afraid to deal with who they are. The placater's problem is that all of the "no's" that are not expressed remain bottled up inside. They build up, and finally they grow into one huge NO! That big NO! can't be talked about or negotiated. In the end, it destroys the relationship.

APPLAUSE!
APPLAUSE!

Arlene has gone out with at least ten different boys this year. All of them are very impressive. John was voted the school's most valuable athlete; Jason is the class scholar; and Martin is the most popular boy in the school. Arlene's boyfriends are not only very impressive, they all seem to treat her in special ways. This year she has already been to several plays, has eaten in some of the best restaurants in town, and has seen just about every movie that has been released.

You might not think that Arlene has a problem—but she does. She gets bored very quickly. She never stays with one boy for very long. And, though she has lots of dates, she often feels lonely and let down.

At the beginning of each new relationship, Arlene becomes excited. Take, for example, the time she went out with Martin. Arlene had been admiring him from a distance for almost a month. When he finally called to ask her out, she was thrilled. She was so excited that she went out and bought new jeans and told all her friends about the date. But, after a month, her enthusiasm for Martin began to wane. Once all the other kids had seen them out together, the thrill was gone.

It was pretty much the same with Jason, John, and all of Arlene's other boyfriends. At first she loved being with them, especially when there were other people around. But when they were alone, Arlene would find little faults that bothered her. For example, she thought that Martin's muscles were overdeveloped and that he looked fat. She decided that John had too many pimples, and that Jason was too quiet. Soon Arlene would start to feel bored, and she'd begin to notice some other boy.

While her friends are sharing and building loving relationships, Arlene keeps starting over. She can't seem to build a relationship she feels happy and comfortable with. Arlene keeps looking for the perfect "Mr. Right." That's why she feels lonely and disappointed.

THE TRAP: Arlene can't help herself. She is compelled to repeat the same patterns over and over again. Despite all her dates, Arlene doesn't feel secure about herself. Secretly she doubts that she has any talents, except for her talent to attract members of the opposite sex.

Arlene would love to be known as the best athlete, best scholar, the best *anything*. Unfortunately, she is unwilling to work to achieve any of these goals. Instead, she has lowered her sights and has become willing to settle for the attention and applause that come from having boyfriends who are the best, the smartest, the most popular. She tries to make herself feel good through association. In other words, by being with boys she admires, she tries to convince herself that she is just like them. She seems to believe that the qualities she wants for herself will magically become hers if she associates with boys who already have them. Being seen in public with her dates is very important to Arlene, because she is trying to win recognition—attention and applause—rather than the love of one person. If the whole world sees her with a boy who is brainy, or athletic, everyone will hold her in high esteem.

Arlene eventually becomes disenchanted with every boy she dates because the boys can't possibly make her feel intelligent, athletic, talented, or extra-special. That's something that Arlene can only do for herself. It's the only way she'll ever free herself from this particular love trap.

THE LOVE JUNKIE

Tony is seeing Alice. He is also going out with Sherry. Every other weekend he dates Mary Ann. He has never actually been out with Lori, but he is planning to ask her very soon. That's how it's always been with him. He's always going out with at least three or four girls at one time. Tony justifies his complicated love life the following way:

"Some guys are jocks, others are scholars. I'm a lover. I love everybody. I'm not using these girls. You see, I really make them happy. . . . Being with just one girl is a hassle. When you have one girlfriend you have to deal with all her problems. When you play it like I do, you never get hung up with all that stuff. If any problems arise, I can drop one girl and have two or three waiting for me. Maybe someday all this will catch up with me, but for now I'm going to continue being a lover, and I'm going to love every minute of it."

THE TRAP: Tony seems to have it all figured out. But whether he knows it or not, he's stuck in a love trap. He is a love junkie. He's in love with the idea of being in love, but all he's ever really experienced is the hunt and the conquest. He has never known true love. Someday Tony will realize that he is missing something in his life. And then he will notice that all the girls he claims to love so much would rather go out with boys who offer them more fulfilling relationships.

Although he talks as if he's the world's greatest lover, inside Tony is very insecure. That's why he has to prove himself over and over again. His insecurities make Tony feel very uncomfortable, so he tries to escape them by chasing after a different girl every few weeks. The more girls he can get to "love" him, the more he thinks he has proven his own worth.

The love junkie is addicted to the conquest and collection of people; he's only high when he thinks he has won a real "trophy." In this way the love junkie is like the applause seeker. And like the applause seeker, the love junkie can only break out of his trap if he comes to terms with his own doubts, fears, and insecurity.

THE HERO
WORSHIPER

Jane hates it when her friends tell her that she is too good for her boyfriend Eric. It's true that he has dropped out of high school and has had some small problems with the police. But these are some of the reasons Jane finds Eric so attractive. She sees him as different from all the other boys she knows—stronger, more independent. In a way, she feels very lucky that he allows her to be his girl.

Jane loves Eric so much that there is absolutely nothing she wouldn't do for him. She runs errands for him, lends him money whenever he needs it, and never says no. When her friends tell her that Eric is just using her and playing her for a sucker, Jane answers by saying, "If he were using me I would definitely know it. It wouldn't feel good. Doing all these nice things for Eric makes me feel wonderful. That's why he always comes back to me."

THE TRAP: Jane has become a hero worshiper—someone who falls in love with a person she believes to be powerful, very much in control of his life, and totally independent. The worshiper overvalues and exaggerates the hero's good qualities. She puts him on a pedestal and proceeds to cater to his every whim. Why does Jane do this? Probably because she feels weak, dependent, and powerless. This makes her long to be with someone who isn't any of these things.

In most cases, the hero worshiper's love hunger is so strong that it distorts her perception of the other person. Despite faults that may be obvious to everyone else, the worshiper sees only her perfect hero. And she does everything to become part of him. She waits on him hand and foot, because she thinks that is the only way to make sure the hero will need her. She thinks it is also the only way that she can prevent him from leaving her.

THE DICTATOR

Eric is a love dictator. It is true that he takes advantage of Jane's willingness to do things for him. He is even a little bit cruel to her. But that's Eric's way. He will do anything that makes him feel good. His philosophy is, "Do whatever you want as long as you don't get caught." Eric figures that as long as Jane wants to worship him, that's just fine. He's always bragging to his friends about how he can get Jane to do anything he wants. One time he asked her to wash and wax his car, and he spent the whole afternoon boasting to anyone who would listen about how he really "wore the pants" in their relationship.

THE TRAP: A love dictator often attracts a hero worshiper. And a love dictator can be a girl or a boy, while boys as well as girls can be hero worshipers. These two types are perfectly suited to each other. On the surface, the dictator seems to be strong and independent. He works very hard to *appear* powerful. But it's all really an attempt to cover up his love hunger. By trying to keep his partner powerless, he is really trying to keep her dependent upon him. In a way, he uses reverse psychology. Instead of admitting his own dependence, he works on keeping his partner dependent. His secret philosophy is, "I may not be lovable, but I'll overcome that by forcing you to love me." The dictator enjoys the powerlessness of his partner. It means that he doesn't have to fear her. By controlling her, the dictator doesn't have to face the thing that frightens him most—being abandoned.

THE GREAT
IMPOSTORS

When Jennifer can't get what she wants from her boyfriend Dan, she begins to cry. Or she gets sick. Sometimes she even gets depressed. It always works. Dan feels guilty and gives in. Here's an example: Jennifer wanted an expensive gold charm for her birthday. Dan said he was sorry, but he couldn't afford it. Jennifer withdrew and went into a deep depression. Her mother even became concerned. Finally, Jennifer told Dan that if she didn't get the charm, life would not be worth living. Dan was so upset that he borrowed the money and presented her with the charm the next day. Jennifer responded by saying, "Well, thanks a lot, but don't expect me to feel better immediately. I'm still in very rough shape because of you."

Jennifer is a great impostor, but she is not the only kind. Ian is also an impostor, though he is the exact opposite of Jennifer. He recently bought his girlfriend Nina a very expensive necklace. Tonight he is taking her to a play, and he has made reservations to take her to one of the best restaurants in town after the show. Ian is constantly showering Nina with presents. All her friends tell Nina that she is very lucky. But for some reason she doesn't always feel that way.

Nina knows that she can never be as good to Ian as he is to her. She couldn't possibly afford to spend as much money on him, or to take him to such terrific places. When Nina tries to explain this to Ian, he replies by saying, "I do all this because I love you. When you're in love you can't do enough for the other person."

Last week something happened that disturbed Nina. She went to a drinking party with Ian. It was the first time for her. Ian had wanted Nina to go out with this crowd for a while, but Nina kept saying no. Finally, she felt that she was being unfair. After all, he had bought her that fabulous necklace, and he had been treating her like a princess. She decided she couldn't refuse him. But Nina was unhappy and uncomfortable at the party. She wound up drinking and didn't feel good about it. The next day Ian sent her flowers. But that didn't make her feel any better. Nina knew she had been conned.

THE TRAP: All great impostors have one thing in common—they work hard to manipulate and trick people into showing love for them. Jennifer uses emotional blackmail. She constantly makes Dan feel that he has made her miserable or even sick. She also uses crying to manipulate him. Dan feels so guilty and so responsible that he gives in every time.

Ian uses a different type of manipulation. He constantly reminds Nina of how much he has done for her and how much she owes him.

Inevitably, Nina gives in when Ian wants to do something she doesn't want to do. It's the only way she knows to repay Ian for his "kindness."

Why do impostors stoop to such dirty tricks with people they claim to love? Because they really don't think anyone could love them any other way. They have such a low opinion of themselves that they believe trickery and manipulation are the only ways to get someone to love them.

Eventually, people like Dan and Nina realize that they are being conned. They see the great impostor for what he or she really is. Unfortunately, great impostors rarely realize why their love relationships fall apart. They just work on more sophisticated tricks to use on their next "true loves."

THE REBEL

Karen is going with Scott. Everyone tells her that he is wrong for her. He's four years older than she is, his religion is different from hers, and, most of all, they have very little in common. They fight quite a bit. Nevertheless, Karen thinks she loves Scott. She may not always *like* him, but she believes she loves him.

There's an element of danger and excitement in Karen's and Scott's relationship. Karen's parents disapprove of Scott, so most of the time she has to sneak out to see him. But she is determined to live her own life—she will go out with anyone she wants, no matter what her parents or her friends say. Karen feels that she is old enough to be treated as an adult. She always says, "In some parts of the world girls my age are mothers." It especially infuriates Karen that no one seems to understand her relationship with Scott. Isn't it true that opposites attract and that love is blind?

THE TRAP: Karen is trying very hard to become an independent person. For her, that means rebelling against her friends and her parents. She believes that by going against the judgment of her parents she will achieve her goal of independence and self-respect. In a way, that's how she got into the relationship with Scott in the first place. Karen knows the kinds of boys her parents would like to see her with, and they are all dull. She is determined to make up her mind and do things her own way. This all sounds okay, except for one thing—Karen is trapped in her own rebellion. She doesn't really love Scott; he is just a symbol for her. He stands for everything that is the opposite of her parents' life and the life they want Karen to lead. Karen wants to be different from her parents—to be free.

In choosing Scott, Karen did not really choose someone to love. She chose someone who would help her to prove that she is different from her parents, her friends, and all the dull boys she meets at school. But that's unfair to Scott. And that may be one reason why he and Karen fight so much. What Karen wants most is to rebel against her present life. This need is so great that it prevents her from really getting to know Scott, and from liking him. The excitement of having to sneak out on dates, the thrill of doing something that is forbidden—and, most of all, the idea that she is a rebel—are what Karen really loves. Scott is just someone who makes it possible for her to do and think these things. If Scott did not seem so "different," or if he wasn't quite so objectionable to her parents, Karen might quickly discover that she was no longer in love.

THE
GOODY-GOODY

Mike is taking Elaine out again tonight. This is the third time in two weeks. Mike doesn't love Elaine—not yet—but he certainly is trying to. It would make everyone so happy. After all, Elaine's parents are best friends with his folks, and everyone says they make a "perfect couple."

When Mike finally agreed to ask Elaine out (his parents had been nagging him about it for months), his dad was pleased with him for the first time. Mike feels good about his father's approval, and he feels good about his mother's eagerness to buy him clothes and give him extra allowance whenever he plans a date with Elaine.

The only thing Mike doesn't feel good about is the time he spends with Elaine. She's quiet, withdrawn, and just not a whole lot of fun to be with. Mike is confused. He's also in a love trap.

THE TRAP: While Karen used Scott to rebel against her parents, Mike is using Elaine to please his. What Mike really wants is his parents' approval—not Elaine. In a way he is using her just as Karen used Scott. She is a symbol to him, not really a person. The sad thing is that Elaine may be using Mike, too, to please *her* parents, or for some other reason. Eventually, Mike and Elaine may convince themselves that they have fallen in love. If this happens, their love trap will be very difficult to escape.

If Mike wants his parents' approval, it's just not fair for him to use another person to get it. Unfortunately, family pressure and social pressure can force people into doing things that are really all wrong for them. Karen, the rebel, is as much a victim of this kind of pressure as Mike, the goody-goody.

THE GOOD NEWS

Now that you've read this, you might realize that some of your friends are in love traps. You might even suspect that you, too, have fallen helplessly into a love trap. Now, here's the good news. There's no need to worry. Everyone experiences love hunger, and as a result even the best of us are trapped by it from time to time. If you can recognize a love trap for what it is, then you are well on your way to getting out of it.

If you take a good honest look at yourself, you will probably find that there is a bit of the clinging vine, the placater, the applause seeker, the hero worshiper, the love dictator, the great impostor, the rebel, and even the goody-goody in you. This is normal, and it doesn't mean that love is hopeless and impossible for you. It does mean that being in love involves some work. In order to have a successful love relationship you have to put in time, patience, understanding, and a lot of honesty (with yourself as well as with your partner!).

An important truth to remember is that love isn't the answer to everything. If you find that a bad case of love hunger has driven you into a love trap, you should ask yourself, "Why? What is happening in my life that has led me into this situation?" And then you should try to do something about it!

Being in love doesn't have to mean being out of control. It's your relationship, and that means you should have a lot to say about every aspect of it. There are many ways to change and form relationships, and to free yourself from love traps. But building a good love relationship takes patience and courage, because love can be a little frightening. In the next chapter you'll find out just why that is.

Love Traps Quiz

Do you suspect that you're in a love trap? This quiz can help you find out if you are. Answer each question by circling T for "true" or F for "false." The key to your answers is at the end of the quiz.

1. When I'm not with the person I love, I feel anxious and insecure.

T   F

2. I prefer to go out with outstanding people—athletes, scholars, or very good-looking people. Others bore me.

T   F

3. No matter how hard I try, I don't think I'll ever be happy with just one person.

T   F

4. Whenever I discover an imperfection in the person I'm dating, I get so turned off that I end the relationship.

T   F

5. I believe that if someone really loves me, he'll do anything I ask him to.

T   F

6. I have always found that there is never a problem between two people that can't be solved with a gift, flowers, or tickets to a show.

T   F

7. Most of my friends don't like the person I love. In a way, that makes dating him even more exciting.

T   F

8. Sometimes I wish I liked the person I'm dating as much as my parents seem to.

T   F

9. No matter how much time we spend together, I never seem able to get enough of the person I love.

T   F

10. It's practically impossible for me to say no to the person I love.

T   F

11. I tend to get bored very quickly with everyone I date.

T   F

12. I only feel good if I'm the boss in a love relationship.

T   F

13. When I'm dating someone who is popular or important, I feel popular and important. But when I'm dating someone who is just ordinary, I feel ordinary, too.

T   F

14. I think that if you really love someone, you should do everything you can for him, even if you really don't want to.

T   F

15. I wouldn't even think of going out with someone my parents didn't approve of.

T   F

16. Although I would do almost anything for the person I love, it's very difficult for me to ask him to do something for me.

T   F

17. When I'm not with the person I love, I always worry that he is with someone else and that he'll stop loving me.

T   F

18. I think that if someone loves me, it's not enough for him just to say it—he should prove it over and over again.

T   F

19. When people I care about caution me

that the person I love is wrong for me, I just assume they are jealous.

T   F

20. I'm always afraid I'll end up with the wrong person; that's why I go out with as many people as I possibly can.

T   F

21. I believe that if two people really love each other, they should never ever fight or really disagree.

T   F

22. Whenever the two of us have a disagreement, I have trouble seeing his point of view, because deep down I believe that if he really loved me he would see things my way.

T   F

23. Secretly I feel very lucky that someone as wonderful as my boyfriend is going out with someone as ordinary as me.

T   F

24. I often do things I don't exactly want to, just because I know it will please my boyfriend.

T   F

25. I'm afraid to even ask my parents if I can go out with someone I think they won't like.

T   F

26. It's always more exciting to go out with someone my parents disapprove of.

T   F

27. If I spend a lot on entertainment and special gifts for my boyfriend, I expect him to do what *I* want.

T   F

Here's the verdict. . . .

If you answered "true" to questions 1, 9, and 17, you might be a clinging vine.

If you answered "true" to questions 2, 4, and 13, ask yourself: "Am I an applause seeker?"

If you said "true" to questions 3, 11, and 20, it's possible that you're a love junkie.

If you answered "true" to questions 14, 16, and 23, you might be caught in the hero worshiper trap.

If you said "true" to questions 5, 12, and 22, you could be a love dictator.

If you said "true" to questions 6, 18, and 27, you may be a great impostor.

If you answered "true" to questions 7, 19, and 26, it's obvious—you're in the rebel trap.

If you answered "true" to questions 8, 15, and 25, you're a goody-goody.

If you said "true" to questions 10, 21, and 24, you're probably a placater.

If your answers don't exactly fit any of these

patterns, then chances are you're not really in a love trap. But you might want to discuss some of your answers with your boyfriend. Even good relationships can stand some improvement. You and your boyfriend might have a lot to talk about—and a few changes to make.

CHAPTER FIVE

Love Ghosts

*E*veryone knows that there's no such thing as ghosts. But don't be so sure about love ghosts. These are not the kind of ghosts that fly around in haunted houses or gather on October thirty-first for Halloween parties. These particular ghosts live in your head. They are a combination of all your conscious and unconscious fears about falling in love and getting close to someone else. Everyone has these ghosts, or fears. And if you could take your ghosts out and compare them to the ghosts of your friends, you would discover that they all look very much alike. That's because everyone is afraid of similar things—especially when it comes to love.

51

Sometimes a love ghost is allowed to grow too big and it can become very powerful. When this happens, fear can actually prevent you from falling in love. It can make you think that love will never happen to you. Love ghosts can also fool you into believing that real love, the kind it seems only Romeo and Juliet had, is free from doubts and uncertainties. Love ghosts can haunt you with fears until you're not sure you even *want* to fall in love. There's only one way to conquer these annoying ghosts: take them out and examine them in the light of day.

THE GHOST OF DEPENDENCY

The ghost of dependency is the fear that if you ever do fall in love you will be so overwhelmed by your need for the other person that you will become completely dependent upon him or her. And no one wants to be completely dependent.

Jacob knows all about this particular love ghost. He is sixteen years old and has had a crush on Holly for almost seven months. Holly isn't going out with anyone special, and Jacob even knows that she likes him a little bit. But he won't ask her out. He's afraid to. It's not that he's afraid she'll say no. He's more afraid she'll say yes, because he fears that if he goes out with Holly, he will fall madly in love with her. So madly in love that nothing else in his life will ever be important again—not basketball, not schoolwork, not his friends, not the bike trip he plans to take in the summer.

Jacob saw what happened when his older brother, Lloyd, fell in love. He dropped out of college, got married, and wound up with a low-paying job and two little babies. Jacob has made up his mind that no girl will take control of *his* future. That's why he's decided to settle for his daydreams about Holly, rather then risk the uncontrollable situation that might develop if he takes her out.

TURNING ON
THE LIGHT

If Jacob were to turn on the light, he'd find that the ghost of dependency is exactly that—a ghost. But Jacob is keeping himself in the dark because he's frightened. Where do his feelings, his fears, come from? They really have more to do with the past than the present.

As a small child, you were extremely dependent. You had no control over your life or even your own body. If your mother wanted you to eat, you did. If she said "Sleep," you did. And if she said you were going to grandmother's house, that's exactly where you went. It's almost impossible to remember what it was like to be so dependent, because it was a long time ago. But, as you can imagine, it wasn't always a comfortable feeling.

Childhood experiences of complete dependency are never really forgotten. They are stored in your unconscious and become sleeping ghosts. But the sleeping ghost of dependency is awakened by the possibility of a new love, because part of being in love and being close means that you have to be somewhat dependent on the other person.

Being dependent on someone as an adult is very different from being dependent as a child. For one thing, you are not out of control the way you were as a baby. You now have an adult mind. You can think for yourself. You can talk, and if you don't like the way things are, you can speak up and change them. But if, like Jacob, you are so busy being afraid, you forget all this. It's just too easy to look at other people's lives and say, "Look at all the horrible things that can happen when you fall in love." That's really a way of saying, "I can't control my life, my feelings, or my relationships." It's also a way of allowing yourself to be haunted by the ghost of dependency.

THE GHOST
OF REJECTION

The ghost of rejection lingers in the back of almost everyone's mind. It's that nagging fear that someone you care about might reject you. Rejection is tough to take. Here's how Jeff describes it:

"There's no way in the world I'm going to take a chance on rejection. Do you think I want to look like a chump or a fool? Sure, I'd love to go out with Jackie, but until I know *for sure* that she will definitely say yes, I'd rather she didn't even know that I like her. I was shot down once by a girl and I was miserable for weeks. I just can't risk that awful feeling ever again."

UNDERSTANDING
REJECTION

The ghost of rejection seems to be the most powerful of all the ghosts. It is an irrational fear that has its roots deep in the unconscious. This ghost gets all of its power by attacking your self-esteem. It convinces you that your self-worth depends entirely upon whether or not the person you are attracted to accepts you.

Jeff is letting his fear of rejection prevent him from exposing his feelings to Jackie, and from asking her out. In this way, Jeff is giving Jackie a lot of power—power she probably doesn't even want. Jeff's self-confidence depends entirely upon what this one girl thinks. If she were to say no, Jeff would hate himself. (That's how the ghost of rejection undermines your self-image.) So instead of risking rejection, Jeff does nothing. The sad truth is that Jeff is making himself unhappy by not asking Jackie out. Even if she did say no, he wouldn't feel any worse than he already does.

It's important to remember that even if one person rejects you, it doesn't mean you're worthless. A feeling of self-worth is something you have to build on your own. It's not something another person can give you. And it's not something anyone else can take away.

THE GHOST OF
ACCEPTANCE

The ghost of acceptance is the opposite of the ghost of rejection. It has to do with the fear that someone else can accept you when you can't accept yourself. It may not sound as if the ghost of acceptance is so terrible or so frightening, but listen to the way Elizabeth explains it:

"There are certain things about myself that I

really don't like—like the fact that I'm ten pounds overweight. Right now I'm also a little broken out on my chin and I know I look just awful. My boyfriend, Rob, never seems to notice these things. He says I'm silly for even worrying about them. But I know what I see when I look in the mirror, and believe me, it turns me off! I can't understand why Rob doesn't feel the same way. He's just as affectionate and loving as he can be. But you know, that makes me feel even worse! I'm always making excuses to Rob whenever he wants to be physically close, or when he wants to take me to a party where I'll be seen by lots of people. Lately, I've been avoiding him altogether. Going out with him only makes me feel guilty that I'm such a mess. He'll notice it eventually, I'm sure of it."

ACCEPTING YOURSELF

The ghost of acceptance tries to prevent you from having a close relationship. It tries to convince you that there are things about you that are so disgusting that no one in the world could really like you, let alone love you. Elizabeth's ghost is trying to convince her that she's so unattractive that nobody could be attracted to her. Rob's feelings for her only make her uneasy. She avoids him because she doesn't understand that Rob's feelings include all of her—the unattractive parts as well as the attractive parts. Elizabeth isn't ready for that sort of love yet, not as long as she remains unaware of the ghost that's hiding inside her—the ghost that makes self-acceptance so difficult for her.

THE GHOST
OF CHANGE

The ghost of change is sneaky. It leads you to believe that just because you like things the way they are, you *won't* like them if they change in any way. This type of fear tells you not to get involved because it will change your life. It also tells you to stay in a relationship you no longer care about, because any change must be for the worse. Dee is being haunted by the ghost of change. Here's how she explains it:

"Bill has been asking me out, but I keep finding excuses to say no. I know all about these relationships. The first thing he'll probably want to do is start seeing me on Friday nights. There goes my skating practice. Then he'll probably want to be with me at least one day on the weekend, and that means giving up my girlfriends or my family. No thank you. He'll probably expect me to go to baseball games, which I hate, and to have dinner at his parents' house, which will only make me nervous. My life is just fine the way it is. Sure I'd like to fall in love. But not if it means I have to change anything about my life."

MAKING CHANGES

The ghost of change has been with Dee since early childhood. Ever since she can remember, she's hated anything unknown. When she was small, she was especially afraid of dark rooms, even if the room was one she knew well, like her own bedroom. It was terrifying to Dee when the lights went out. There in the dark, she would imagine that all sorts of monsters and snakes were hiding everywhere. When the lights went back on, she was surprised and relieved. She felt safe only when she could see everything that was around her.

Dee is seventeen now. She has conquered her fear of the dark, but she is still very afraid of the unknown. She thinks that accepting a date with Bill means her life must change all at once. And what's worse, Dee believes that all changes are something to be afraid of. Maybe Dee isn't ready for love yet. Maybe Bill isn't the right boy for her. But Dee's idea that her life should never change could prevent her from *ever* meeting the right boy.

It's true that change can be upsetting, even a little scary. But growing up involves change.

And those changes don't stop when you're twenty-one—they just keep on happening. The ghost of change can frighten you into thinking that you have no control over the changes in your life, and that they are all for the worse. Don't believe it.

CHECKING YOUR
HOUSE FOR
GHOSTS

Love ghosts aren't the only things that prevent love from happening. There are other realities that can be obstacles to closeness with someone else. But before you feel sorry for yourself because you've never fallen in love (or because love has never been returned when you did feel it), take an honest look at yourself and find out if you're being haunted by love ghosts.

Maybe a dependency ghost is whispering in your ear, telling you that if you allow yourself to care about anyone he will take over your whole life and then hurt you. Or maybe the ghost of rejection is warning you not to make the first move because you're sure to be shot down. Perhaps the ghost of acceptance is telling you to stay home from that party or to avoid that special someone because he won't be able to accept things about you that you can't accept. Or maybe the ghost of change is haunting you with the fear that your whole life will be transformed by love and is urging you to resist change because all change is bad.

If love is frightening to you, you're probably being haunted by love ghosts. But remember, you *can* overcome these ghosts. Make yourself take them out and examine them in the light of day. That involves being honest with yourself, and being honest isn't always so easy. You may discover that you don't really want to ask yourself questions about your fears. But it pays off in the end.

CHAPTER SIX

The Dating Game

*I*f dating is supposed to be so much fun, why doesn't it always feel that way? There's no doubt about it—there are times when everyone feels awkward, embarrassed, and uncomfortable. Anyone who's ever gone out on a date knows what agony it can be. First there's waiting by the telephone, or trying to get up the courage to make a call. Then, what about all the preparation? You worry about what to wear, where you'll go, and whether you're going to make a total fool of yourself. Finally there's the date itself—it's not easy knowing what to say and when not to say anything at all. Afterward, it can be nerve-wracking to wonder if he'll call again or if he really did have a good time with you. And what about those dates who never do call back, or who are always busy when you call? The question is, why do most people think of dating as a "game," when it's really hard work?

SOCIAL STUDIES

Maybe no one ever told you this before, but, though going out on dates can be fun, it's also a form of social studies. Not the kind you learn in school—the kind you learn when you go out to dinner with a boy you hardly know, or go with a guy your friend said was terrific to a school dance or a movie.

Dating involves learning through experience. Dates are one very good way to study different social situations. At the same time that you're eating all that pizza and making all that small talk, you're learning what works on a date and what doesn't. You're discovering the type of boy who attracts you and the type who definitely does not. You're getting practice in relating to boys on a one-to-one basis. That's why dating is important. But it's also why you may well dread going out with different people.

Each date offers new challenges and new obstacles to overcome. Let's say you're just learning about football so you can have a terrific conversation with that cute quarterback—and the president of the chess club asks you out. Or you've finally figured out a way to get that shy boy to talk, but no matter how many hints you manage to drop, he doesn't ask you to the spring dance. When things like this happen, it's easy to get discouraged, throw up your hands, and say, "I give up!"

Obviously, if you only go out with one person, dating will be less of a hassle. An exclusive relationship may seem very, very desirable to you. But suppose an exclusive relationship isn't possible or isn't what you need right now? What then?

PLAYING THE FIELD

You've undoubtedly heard the expression "I'm just playing the field." But it's confusing. Just what does it really mean? Does playing the field mean you're "fickle," a shallow person who just wants to be with a different boy every night and doesn't care about anyone? Or can it mean that you're learning more about people, yourself, and the opposite sex?

Laura isn't sure what playing the field means, either. And these days she feels as if she's just struck out. You see, Kelly finally asked her out. They had a wonderful time. He kissed her good night and said he'd call. And he did—only he didn't call Laura. He called Betsey, someone who goes to the same school but isn't in Laura's crowd. When Laura found out, she was furious. How could Kelly do such a thing? That's when Laura's friend Monica told her about playing the field.

Monica explained that Kelly dated lots of girls. He didn't like to be with the same girl all the time. "He's known for that," Monica said. "Don't take it personally." But Laura couldn't understand her friend's advice. She felt betrayed, used. She was sure Kelly hated her.

Laura hadn't struck out at all. But she *was* way out in left field. And then, just when she was feeling her lowest, Kelly called. He was asking her to the Senior Dance. Laura didn't know what to say. She wasn't even sure if Kelly was serious. "What about Betsey?" she asked.

"Oh, I went to the movies with her last week," Kelly replied, "but I'd like to take *you* to the dance.

"Does that mean it's all over between you and Betsey?" Laura asked.

Kelly paused. There were a few seconds of awful silence on the phone. "It never really began," he answered.

GETTING YOUR
SIGNALS CROSSED

From Kelly's tone of voice, Laura got the message that she had a lot of social studying to catch up on. She knew when she spoke to him that Kelly wasn't a user, a cheater, or a playboy. He'd had a good time with Laura. But that didn't mean he was ready to see her exclusively. One date just meant they were friends. They'd had fun. They'd learned something about each other. For Kelly, that didn't mean it was wrong or disloyal to ask Betsey out.

Laura got her signals crossed. She thought that the good-night kiss, the promise that he'd call, also meant that Kelly wouldn't kiss or call anyone else. This kind of thing happens a lot. It's not always clear just what a date means. And maybe that's because for some people it means one thing, and for others, it means something else entirely.

DOING YOUR
HOMEWORK

Maybe you think the expression "playing the field" shouldn't apply to someone like Kelly. Maybe you think that Kelly sounds like a nice guy who just wants to meet different girls. Maybe you think the expression "playing the field" makes it sound as if someone is having fun at another person's expense. As you just saw, that really wasn't the case with Kelly. And it isn't the case with Hillary, either.

Hillary just broke up with Derek. They had been going together for six months. For Hillary, that was long enough. Now she wants to meet other boys. She wants to "date around" before she gets involved in a heavy, exclusive relationship again. But the boys Hillary has been going out with think she's looking for that special "one" again.

When Hillary went out with Floyd, she had a nice time. She felt so comfortable with him that she told him how glad she was that she and Derek had broken up. She said it felt good to have some "breathing room" again. Floyd smiled and said he understood. The next day he called her. And he called her the day after that. Then he found out that Hillary had accepted a date with Matt for that Saturday. He felt hurt, rejected, and angry.

Like Laura, Floyd got his signals crossed. And he didn't do his homework; he didn't study the situation and get a clear picture of what was going on. When he called Hillary the day after their date, Floyd didn't ask her out again. He just assumed that they would be going out together—or at least that Hillary wouldn't be going out with anyone else. Maybe Hillary should have explained her situation and feelings to Floyd; or maybe he should have asked her.

Every person and every crowd is different. In some places, if you go out with someone once, you're considered a couple. In other crowds, it may take a lot of dates before two people are considered boyfriend and girlfriend. The important thing is to do your homework. If you're not sure what a date means (can you accept a date with someone else without stepping on anyone's toes?), it's best to get things straight right away. After all, social studies means thinking about the date and studying the situation. If Floyd had done his homework, he would have remembered what Hillary had told him about Derek. He would have remembered that she'd said she was relieved not to be going with one boy, and that she had felt suffocated and hemmed in by her relationship with Derek. By calling her every day and expecting her to be his girl right after she broke up with someone else, Floyd was not only forgetting to do his homework, he was forgetting that Hillary needed to play the field for a while. If Floyd keeps up this possessive behavior, Hillary might just forget she ever met him.

WHAT'S FAIR AND WHAT'S NOT?

Although Kelly and Hillary were both playing the field, they were also playing by the rules. Kelly asked someone else out, but it wasn't a close friend of Laura's, and he never promised Laura that he wouldn't date other girls. Hillary didn't cheat on or betray Floyd when she went out with someone else. But there *is* such a thing as "cheating," "using," and "being fickle."

Nola went out with Sal three times. He is the star of the track team and someone all the girls would like to date. Sal was crazy about Nola. After their third date, he asked her if she was going out with anyone else. Nola *was* seeing someone from another school—someone even more popular than Sal. But she was afraid that if Sal found out about Rick, he might never ask her out again.

Nola was in a bind. She didn't want to lose Sal *or* Rick. She wasn't ready to make a choice—she was having too much fun. So instead of explaining things to Sal she lied. She said that she wasn't dating anyone else. That made Sal feel good, because he knew from past experience that he had trouble dealing with jealousy. He preferred to date one girl exclusively—that was his way of keeping his jealous feelings under control. And for Sal, it was a good way. But Nola didn't know anything about this, and she didn't think to ask.

Nola thought that if she only had a little more time, she could decide between Sal and Rick and no one would know the difference. It might have worked. But then Sal and Rick both asked her out for the same night. When she tried to rearrange things, she discovered that Sal and Rick both had family obligations on the other days. Nola had to make a choice, and she accepted the date with Rick. She was afraid to tell Sal that she couldn't go out with him because she had a date with someone else, so, instead, she said that she had to stay home and baby-sit for her little brother.

The trouble began that Saturday night when Sal decided to call Nola just to say hi. Nola's mother answered the phone and forgot what Nola had told her to say "in case" Sal called. Nola's mother simply told Sal that Nola was out. Sal immediately knew that Nola had lied to him about staying home to baby-sit. And, though he didn't know it then, he soon found out that she had cheated, too.

Sal never waited to hear Nola's explanations. He knew she had treated him unfairly, and he didn't want to stick around and be hurt any more.

Nola really did cheat—not just by going out with someone else, but by not being straight with Sal to begin with. If she had explained that yes, she *was* dating someone else, but that she wasn't ready to go exclusively with him, Sal might have listened. She could have also told him that she liked him a great deal, but that she wanted to have some time before she decided not to date other boys. Sal might have been able to live with the truth, or he might have said "forget it." One thing's for sure—Sal wasn't able to live with a lie, and Nola not only lost Sal, she lost his trust as well.

PLAYING BY
THE RULES

Even though the rules for dating aren't written anywhere, everyone knows the difference between a lie and the truth, between acting in good faith and cheating. Sometimes, by talking it out, you can come to see the other person's side. Maybe if Nola and Sal had discussed it, Sal would have seen that Nola was afraid of telling the truth because she was afraid she'd lose him.

The ball is in Nola's court now. And if she wants to win Sal back and regain his trust, she has only one option—playing by the rules.

BEING SENSIBLE

Kelly, Hillary, and Nola all needed to date more than one person. They felt unready for exclusive relationships. All three needed time to study different social situations, to learn more about themselves and the opposite sex. And that's fine. But for many people, playing the field just doesn't feel right. You may feel that if you're dating one person and then accept a date with another, you're cheating. You may also feel that it's perfectly natural to be upset if you discover that the boy you've been dating is dating another girl as well. Maybe you think, deep down, that playing the field shouldn't be allowed. But since it is, here are a few pointers that will help make playing the field a lot more bearable:

Play by the rules. If you feel as though you'd like to date more than one boy, don't try to lie or cover up. Be honest. Remember how Nola lost out when she lied and cheated on Sal!

Know yourself. You may be able to date two people at once and not feel the least bit guilty about it. On the other hand, dating more than one boy may make you feel uncomfortable and even dishonest. Deciding what's right for you takes time. But it's your decision, so be sure to make one you can live with.

Don't jump to conclusions. If the boy you're dating wants to play the field, don't jump to the conclusion that he doesn't care about you, or that he never wants to date you again. Maybe there are reasons for his decision. He might have broken up with someone recently, or he might feel that he isn't ready for a steady relationship. Try and find out why he wants to date other girls before you lose yourself in a sea of anger and self-pity.

Avoid making demands. Don't overwhelm or suffocate the boy you're dating—especially if he wants to play the field. Watch out for sneaky manipulations on your part that may try and force him to date only you. Don't coerce him into promising that he won't see any other girls when it's clear that this is something he wants and needs to do.

Don't get in over your head! If you are dating a boy who is dating other girls, beware of getting too emotionally involved! Remember that although he likes you, he also likes to be free and to meet other girls. Falling too deeply for this type of boy, at a time when he is playing the field, can make you feel that you've been played for a fool.

PROBLEMS, SETBACKS, AND SOLUTIONS

Up till now, this book has talked mostly about the things that can prevent you from falling in love—love traps, love hungers, love ghosts—and about the possible perils of the dating game. But what happens when you've triumphed over all the obstacles? When you've found someone who shares your feelings—someone who is not a fantasy, a symbol, or an illusion?

First, you'll probably feel totally terrific. Love is like that. It makes some people light-headed and giddy. Other people find that they can't eat or sleep. And still others discover that food tastes even better and dreams are sweeter. But no one in love feels this good all the time. That's because every love relationship—even the best of them—has occasional setbacks and problems. After all, love involves people, and people are never perfect.

Everyone who has ever been in love has experienced doubts, angers, jealousies, and conflicts. The old saying, "True love never runs smooth," isn't far from the truth. Feelings like these are part of love. They don't always mean that your love isn't real or that your relationship can't be improved. But working it out takes time and patience—and in the next chapters you'll learn how.

CHAPTER SEVEN

The Boundaries of Love

There's a romantic song that says, "There's nothing in the world I wouldn't do for love." That line sounds lovely, and it rhymes with the lines that precede and follow it. But it also seems to say that when you're *really* in love you forget about everything you want to do and agree to anything the person you love requests. Most of all, it suggests that if you are *really* in love, you will lose your self. This certainly seems poetic and romantic—but can it be true? If you give up your self, who can the person you love be in love with?

Remember, your self is the most wonderful thing you can share with another person. And sharing does *not* mean the same thing as for-feiting. Love does have boundaries. Setting those boundaries is a challenge made for two.

SELFISHNESS VS. SELFLESSNESS

Have you ever taken part in a conversation that sounded like this one?

BARRY: Where do you want to go tonight?

ENID: I don't know, wherever you want to go.

BARRY: Why do I always have to decide every-thing?

ENID: You don't. It's just that I love you, so anything you like to do, I like to do.

Or like this one?

EDDIE: Jay and Marie are going to the movies tonight. They asked me if we wanted to go, so I said we would.

SUSAN: How could you say yes without asking me?

EDDIE: Aw, come on! Why do I have to ask you about every little thing? If you really loved me you'd like to go out with my friends.

In the first conversation, Enid is being *selfless*. In the second conversation, Eddie is being *selfish*. Both attitudes can be destructive even to the best relationships.

By being selfless, Enid is forfeiting her self. She hasn't separated her needs and her likes from Barry's needs and likes. Like a clinging vine, she is hoping that if she just follows Barry's lead, their love will last. But if you've ever experienced this kind of selfless love, you know how irritating it can be. Originally, Barry fell in love with Enid because she was like him in many ways—but she was also different. The important thing was that Barry and Enid were never *identical*. That's what made their love so exciting and so much fun.

Eddie is being *selfish*. He is insisting that if Susan loves him, she should want to do the same things he wants to do and should like the same people he likes. After all, Eddie believes (and here comes the classic persuader), "If you really loved me you'd . . ."

Being in love doesn't mean you have to be selfless; neither does it mean you can be selfish. There is a middle ground between the two. Barry and Enid and Susan and Eddie need to find that middle ground. You and the person you love will need to discover it, too.

THE URGE TO
MERGE VS.
THE SENSE TO
SEPARATE

The famous psychologist and author Erich Fromm once said, "When two people are in love they become one. At the same time they must remain two." This sounds simple enough, but if you give it some thought, you'll see that it is really very complex. When you are in love, you experience two opposite forces—the urge to merge, and the urge to remain separate.

Sometimes, like Enid, you want to do whatever the person you love wants to do. You want to be together and experience that wonderful feeling of oneness. But at other times, you need (and want) to separate yourself from the other person. This does not mean you are selfish. It means you are sensible. Having the sense to separate helps you to remain in contact with reality and with your self. Unfortunately, it's sometimes easy to forget all about your self.

SEPARATE
AND EQUAL

Why does Enid agree with Barry all the time? It's not because she always wants to do what he wants to do. It's because she is secretly afraid that if she doesn't agree with Barry, he won't love her. It's also because she's afraid that being a separate person means she and Barry must separate.

Enid would like to believe that her love for Barry is so deep and so real that there is no sacrifice she wouldn't make for him. But Barry doesn't *want* Enid to make sacrifices. He wants her to be separate from him in some ways and together with him in others. He wants her to retain her self, but to share it with him at the same time. Barry is beginning to find Enid's selfless behavior annoying. He doesn't like to argue, but he doesn't want Enid to agree with him and to defer to him all the time, either.

Enid is afraid that if she expresses her needs and desires she will seem selfish and pushy. She's also afraid that this might result in a power struggle and in the sort of fights her own parents have all the time. Enid doesn't really believe that she can be separate from Barry and still be equal to him. She's afraid that this is what will happen if they disagree:

BARRY: Where do you want to go tonight?

ENID: I'd like to go to the rock concert at the auditorium.

BARRY: You know how much I hate those concerts and all the crowds.

ENID: You're just being silly! Come on, let's go—please.

BARRY: No way! If I'm so silly you can just go without me, and you can go without me to the dance next week, too!

HOW BOUNDARIES WORK

Personal boundaries are like borders. Borders separate one state from another, one country from another; boundaries separate one person from another. We draw boundaries around ourselves when we say things like, "I need," "I want," "I like," "It's my opinion that," "My feeling is that." Boundaries are important in all relationships. They help you to define your self, and they let other people know more about who you are and what you need and expect.

Enid needs to learn how to establish her own boundaries, and how to respect Barry's. She needs to understand that these boundaries will enrich her relationship with Barry, rather than impoverish it. Here's another version of their conversation, but this time Enid's attitude is different:

BARRY: Where do you want to go tonight?

ENID: I'd like to go to the rock concert at the auditorium.

BARRY: You know how much I hate those concerts.

ENID: I know you hate them, but I don't understand why.

BARRY: Everything is so crowded and noisy and tense. We don't really get to be together at all.

ENID: I see what you mean, but I'd still like to go. Tell you what—I'll go to the second performance with some of my girlfriends. Let's figure out what we'd both enjoy doing tonight.

BARRY: Okay. How about a romantic walk in the park—just the two of us?

ENID: That sounds great to me!

WHAT'S DIFFERENT?

In this conversation Enid did not give in to Barry. But she did not force her wishes on him, either. She listened, and she and Barry were able to compromise. Enid found a middle ground between being selfish and being selfless. And it worked. Barry felt even more in love with her because they had found a solution that suited both of them.

Boundaries don't have to result in power struggles. They are not brick walls. And they don't have to be permanent. Maybe, at some point, Enid can help Barry to feel more relaxed and to enjoy rock concerts. But if she can't, then that's just something that will make them different from each other. It doesn't have to stand between them, and it doesn't have to be a source of conflict.

WHEN BOUNDARIES OVERLAP

Enid and Barry were able to reach a satisfactory compromise during their last conversation. But things don't always work out so neatly. What if Enid and Barry were unable to find a middle ground—a place where their needs and desires overlapped? Suppose their conversation went like this?

BARRY: Where do you want to go tonight?

ENID: To the rock concert at the auditorium.

BARRY: I hate those concerts!

ENID: Well, what would you like to do?

BARRY: I'd like to go to the basketball game.

ENID: Forget it! Those games are so boring—I just hate them.

BARRY: I give up! We can never agree on anything.

Sounds frustrating, doesn't it? But it's also very real. Another thing that's real is that Barry and Enid don't *always* disagree. Just sometimes. Maybe this time Enid could give in and go to the game, or maybe Barry could try going to the concert. Or they could choose to do something else entirely—maybe something they did together in the past that they both enjoyed. They could even decide to go their separate ways for one evening. The point is that Enid and Barry both need to let each other know what they want and who they are. Each also needs to listen to and consider the needs and desires of the other. Like all couples, Barry and Enid need to be able to say no to each other, as well as yes. They need to be able to reach compromises that are based on understanding and respect for each other's identities.

WHEN SOMEONE
OVERSTEPS
YOUR BOUNDARIES

Very often people in love ask each other to make sacrifices. Sometimes those sacrifices seem fair or just plain necessary. But sacrifices should be made by choice. When you are forced into making a sacrifice, you don't really give *to* the other person—you give *in*.

Selfishness is the opposite of selflessness, and, of course, it can be just as irritating. Remember when Eddie made plans without consulting Susan? When she objected, he answered, "If you really loved me you'd like my friends, too."

Eddie was using a common ploy to try to manipulate Susan. Whether he knew it or not, he was trying to make Susan feel guilty. She might have thought, "Gee, I do love Eddie, and if I love him I should go along with him." In some cases Susan might be right to think this. But in this particular case, Eddie was forcing Susan to base *her* love on *his* needs. He was saying that Susan had no right to any personal boundaries, and that he and Susan were one person. Unfortunately for Susan, that one person was Eddie!

Everyone tends to be selfish at one time or

another, and people in love are no exception. But too much selfishness may indicate that you don't see the self in someone else. And that's not love—that's self-involvement.

SELFISHNESS HURTS

When someone steps on your foot, it hurts. Perhaps it was a harmless accident, but that doesn't make it less painful. The same thing happens when the person you love ignores your boundaries. He steps on a part of you—and that hurts.

You might believe that it's easier to give in to selfishness than it is to prevent it. Let's go back to the example of Eddie and Susan again. Eddie accepted an invitation without consulting Susan. He acted selfishly, and Susan let him know it. Then Eddie tried to make her feel guilty by saying, "If you *really* loved me, you'd . . ."

What Susan does next is very important. If she simply says "okay" to Eddie, she is giving up an important part of her self. She is letting Eddie overstep or ignore her personal boundaries. If this giving up and giving in continues, Susan will eventually find herself thinking, "Eddie takes me for granted. He bosses me around. I feel like a doormat. I exist only to agree with him."

No one likes it when her toes have been stepped on, when her boundaries have been ignored, or when she thinks she has been taken for granted. If resentment at this kind of treatment is not expressed, it doesn't disappear. It just gets buried. But eventually, resentments do break through the surface. And when this happens, they can destroy even the "truest" love. That's why it's so important to acknowledge that it's not selfish to have a self. It hurts when the person you love forgets that. It isn't always simple to do, but if you want your love to last, you need to balance your rights as an individual with your needs as a couple.

EMOTIONAL BRUISES

Susan has a problem. She is avoiding her responsibility to her self and to her relationship with Eddie. When someone hurts you physically, you can show him the bruise. He will see that he has been too rough and understand that, in the future, he must be more careful. But emotional bruises are invisible. It's up to you to let people know when they have been careless or rough with your feelings. Letting them know isn't always something you might want to do; it can be difficult or even embarrassing. You might also be afraid that it will result in a fight and even more emotional bruises.

There are some ways of sharing your feelings

that are bound to be more successful than others. The more you practice the better you'll get at expressing your feelings, and the fewer emotional bruises you'll have to bear. Let's see how Susan and Eddie might have continued their conversation. . . .

TELLING

One way to let someone you care about know that he has overstepped important boundaries is to tell him. That sounds easy, but it can result in some real problems. When Eddie told Susan that he had already made plans with Jay and Marie, she might have answered like this:

SUSAN: Eddie, I can't believe how inconsiderate and selfish you are! How dare you make plans without asking me?

It wouldn't take much guesswork to predict how Eddie would reply—probably like this:

EDDIE: How dare *you* tell *me* about being selfish and inconsiderate! What about the time when you . . . ?

If this conversation really took place, Susan and Eddie would be in for a long and upsetting argument. And the argument would not bring them closer; it might even lead them to break up. That's what Susan is afraid of, and that's why she decided to keep quiet and not make a big thing out of it. But telling is only one way to talk to the person you love. There's another way, and it works much better.

SHARING VS. TELLING

If you want to get an important message across, you can tell a person what you think of him; or you can share your feelings about a particular situation. Sharing is better than telling. That's because when you simply *tell* another person something, he feels he is being attacked. Telling usually involves putting someone down, or giving him advice on how to behave. Either way you make him feel like a child. Then *you* are bruising *him* emotionally. Before you know it, you're involved in an emotional fistfight. And emotional punches can ache for a long time. It's hard to forget when someone says cruel things to you, even in the heat of anger.

If Susan were to share her feelings with Eddie, instead of telling him how inconsiderate and selfish he is, the conversation would sound something like this:

SUSAN: Eddie, when you make plans without consulting me I feel that I'm unimportant to you and that I'm being taken for granted.

EDDIE: I'm sorry, I didn't want to make you feel that way. I guess I wasn't considering you very much. What can we do about it now?

Can you see the difference? This time Susan didn't tell Eddie how selfish and bossy he was. She didn't give him advice or put him down. That made it easier for Eddie to hear what Susan was saying and to respond calmly. He didn't feel he was being attacked, so he didn't have to try to defend himself. *There is a difference between telling and sharing.* Here are some more examples:

TELLING	SHARING
"Will you hurry up and make up your mind where we're going to go tonight?"	"I'd like to go to the movies; what about you?"
"When are you going to stop being so inconsiderate?"	"I feel taken for granted when you do that."
"You're so insecure. You have to follow me everywhere."	"I'd like to go there by myself."
"Don't you realize that no one goes to this place anymore?"	"I'd like to try going somewhere else."
"You're a liar! I can't believe a word you say."	"It's important for me to know the truth about all of this."
"You have the creepiest friends!"	"I'd rather not go out with them. Let's double with someone else."

TELLING	SHARING
"You rat! No one treats me like that and gets away with it!"	"My feelings are hurt, and right now I'm angry and confused."
"You talk too much. When are you going to learn how to keep your mouth shut?"	"I get so frustrated when you interrupt me."

LOVE AND
SELF-RESPECT

Sharing your feelings and needs instead of telling the other person how he should act will improve your love relationship. It will also help you to maintain your self-respect. The more you practice sharing instead of telling, the more you will see what an effective technique it is. But there will always be those times when nothing seems to work.

Suppose you do share your feelings and the person you love doesn't respond? Suppose he tries to persuade you to do something—or tries to talk you out of something you think is important—by using expressions like this?

"Oh, don't be so sensitive!"
"Can't you do this one little thing for me?"
"Oh, come on—please!"

In cases like this, it's up to you to protect your personal boundaries and your self-respect.

But you'll still have to do it *without attacking the person you love.*

It isn't always easy to take a firm stand, but after a while it becomes necessary. Otherwise, you might find that the person you love has become bossy, unattractive, and boring to you. You might even feel bad about yourself—you might think it's all your fault, or that you were never really in love to begin with. These feelings can be confusing and upsetting.

Let's say you're in one of those bad situations—you've tried to share your feelings, but you just don't seem to be getting through. You might be tempted to threaten, whine, or cry. But that won't help. Expressions like these will:

"I'm sorry, but I care too much about myself to go along with that."

"I feel this issue is too important to say yes or no right away. I need some time to think about it."

"I just wouldn't feel comfortable if I did that."

"We'll just have to disagree about this and let it pass until we can come up with a solution that works for both of us."

"This means a lot to me right now. Please don't try to talk me out of it."

YOU + ME = WE

It takes two separate people to make one loving couple. You and the person you love may not always want different things, but frequently you

will. Understanding that when you love someone, you don't lose your *self*, takes time and
practice. Everyone would like to have the type
of relationship where there are no disagree-
ments, no dull moments, no uncomfortable incidents, and a guaranteed "happily ever after."
But real life doesn't work that way. And reality
is what makes love so exciting and full of
surprises.

Think about the person you love. Think about
how he is different from you and how you are
the same. You probably love him for his differ-
ences as well as for his similarities. Help him
retain his individuality by letting him know
more about yours. Boundaries are the outlines
you draw so that the person you love can see
your self, know it, and love it. Drawing boundaries doesn't mean that you are selfish or selfless. It means you are a whole person, not an
extension of someone else. Remember, it takes
two whole people—a "me" and a "you" to equal
a "we."

CHAPTER EIGHT

Jealousy

Some people call it the "green-eyed monster"; others think it's cute; and still others would do anything rather than admit they're feeling it. But jealousy is part of everyone's emotional self.

It's generally assumed that jealousy is unexplainable and uncontrollable. But that's not really the case at all. Jealousy can be explained and understood. And, if you're really determined, you can *control* your jealousy!

THE RECIPE FOR
JEALOUSY

Jealousy doesn't just happen. It's a concoction you create—and the recipe is really very simple:

JEALOUSY =   one part anger
one part fear
one part rejection
one part shame

These ingredients are heated over the flame of passion, stirred up by suspicion, and thickened by dishonesty. But beware! The whole mixture is certain to boil over if not carefully watched and understood.

BUBBLE,
BUBBLE . . .

In order for jealousy to boil over, the ingredients have to be assembled and the conditions must be just right. Here's a perfect example of what can happen:

Martin and Deena are going together. They're at a party. Martin begins to talk with Lucy. Deena notices this out of the corner of her eye.

Then she notices that Martin and Lucy have moved to a corner of the room and that they are whispering and laughing. Deena stands in another corner of the room and watches Martin and Lucy very closely. Several people try to engage Deena in conversation, but she is too busy watching, and trying to listen, and stirring up her jealousy.

Finally, music for a slow dance comes on. Deena marches over to Martin and insists that he dance with her. While they're dancing, Martin says, "Lucy just told me the most amazing story."

"I don't want to hear it. I'm not interested in anything *she* has to say!" says Deena (practically shouting).

"What's got into you?" asks Martin.

"What's got into *me*? You bring me to this party, then you spend the entire evening talking to someone else. It's as if I don't even exist!" shouts Deena.

"What are you talking about?" asks Martin. "All I did was talk to Lucy for a few minutes!"

"Well, that's enough. I want to go home!" answers Deena.

"I can't stand your senseless jealousy anymore!" shouts Martin.

"*I'm not jealous!* I just can't stand this stupid party one more second and I want to leave right now!" screams Deena.

JEALOUS?
WHO, ME?

Mark's and Deena's story is a classic. It shows precisely how jealousy can ruin an evening—and a relationship.

Sometimes jealousy can make you so angry and so insecure that you make a fool of yourself. You can't eat or sleep. You find yourself following the person you love, trying to catch him betraying your trust; maybe you even wind up in a fight with someone you think is threatening your relationship. Jealousy is so uncomfortable that, for most people, covering it up seems like the best way to deal with it.

Deena was obviously jealous of Lucy, but instead of being honest about her feelings and discussing them with Martin, she answered with the traditional cover-up: "Jealous? Who, me?" Here are some other cover-ups that might sound familiar to you:

"I'm just not the jealous type."

"I'm too sure of myself to stoop to jealousy!"

"It's wrong to feel jealous, so I never do."

"Anyone who ever gets jealous is just immature."

"Why should I be jealous? I don't even care about him."

"I'm not jealous. I just can't stand the way she acts around boys."

Obviously, it's impossible to get to the bottom of your jealous feelings if you deny that you have them. It's even more difficult if you think that being jealous means you are sick, immature, or insecure. Remember, jealousy is a combination of anger, fear, rejection, and shame. And these are emotions that *everyone*, male or female, young or old, experiences at various times.

THE ANGER

Maybe you're asking yourself what jealousy has to do with anger. After all, what is there to be angry about? Let's take a look at Deena and figure out why she's feeling the way she is.

Deena's jealousy began when she noticed that Martin and Lucy were talking. It began with her anger. She was furious that Martin was spending time with another girl. She felt that if he'd brought her to a party, he should spend all his time with her. Is that unreasonable? Not if Martin had agreed to it beforehand. But Martin and Deena had never made an agreement like that. (Perhaps, if they had, the incident never would have happened.) Martin and Deena went to the party to spend time together, but they also intended to spend time with other people—at least Martin did. All this sounds very reasonable, so why is Deena so angry?

THE FEAR

Deena's anger is easier to understand when we see that it plays into her fear. She's not just angry because Martin talked to another girl for a few minutes. She's angry because she's afraid that Martin might be interested in Lucy. She's afraid that he will find Lucy prettier, funnier, and smarter than she is. Maybe Martin and Lucy have already begun falling in love, right before her very eyes! Deena is angry, but she is also afraid, and these two emotions are beginning to form a hot and spicy combination.

THE REJECTION

Along with the fear and the anger, Deena is feeling something else—rejection. Just the thought that Martin might find someone else more attractive hurts Deena a lot. To Deena, being rejected is the worst thing that could ever happen. It's so unbearable that she can't even let herself think about it; she covers up her worries about rejection with other feelings. All Deena really wants is to get close to Martin and show him how much she cares about him. But her anger, her fear, and her worries about rejection combine to make her hostile, and then she pushes Martin further away.

THE SHAME

If Deena is feeling all this, why doesn't she just tell Martin about it, instead of yelling at him and forcing him to take her home? Easy. Deena is ashamed of her feelings. Nothing could get her to admit that she's angry and afraid, feels rejected, and (most of all) cares enough about Martin to be jealous. That's too bad, because if Martin doesn't know that Deena's actions are a result of her caring for him so deeply, he can't be expected to respond to her in a caring way.

Instead of explaining to Martin why his attentions to Lucy make her so uneasy, Deena chooses to deny everything, claim she isn't jealous at all, and force Martin to take her directly home. The sad thing is, it's likely that the more Martin tries to find out about Deena's attitude, the more she will deny the truth. After a while, Martin may begin to think that he doesn't know Deena at all. And that's how two people in love can become two strangers.

THE JEALOUSY GAME

If Deena doesn't learn how to cope with her jealousy and how to discuss it with Martin, she will probably wind up playing the jealousy game.

There are many variations on this time-worn game. Here are a few of the most common ones:

> The Private Eye
> The Direct Attack
> Self-Blame
> Reverse Psychology
> Exclusive Ownership

Most people who experience jealousy but try to cover it up or deny it have played (or have attempted to play) a jealousy game. And even though the outcome is almost always disastrous, the players rarely become discouraged. Maybe that's because they think that if they play the jealousy game long enough, they will become experts. Maybe they're convinced that experts at the jealousy game win. But that's where they're wrong. The more expert they become, the more they stand to lose. Here are a few examples:

PAUL THE PRIVATE EYE

Until recently, Paul was a very busy guy. He was following Robin everywhere. *He* never wanted to be accused of being jealous, of imagining things, or of being insecure. He was too cool, too smart, for that. So instead he put all his efforts into collecting "evidence" and building an airtight case against Robin. He watched her at parties, and at lunchtime in the cafeteria. He called her at different times every evening to see if she was home. He turned into a regular Sherlock Holmes.

Paul didn't want to have to admit his worries and fears, so he tried to prove that Robin really was disloyal to him, and that what he was feeling wasn't jealousy at all—it was righteous indignation.

For a while, no matter how hard he worked at building a case against Robin, Paul couldn't get enough evidence for a "conviction." But instead of feeling relieved that Robin was apparently loyal to him after all, Paul thought he should work even harder. He became convinced that he'd missed something.

Then Robin caught on to Paul's undercover work. And she told him that she thought his checking up on her all the time meant that he was distrustful of her. This was just the kind of evidence Paul needed! He thought, "Why would Robin get so angry at me if she had nothing to hide? So Paul redoubled his efforts. He began to call Robin's friends, and he showed up late at parties, hoping to catch Robin with someone else.

Finally, Robin took Paul aside. She told him that she didn't want to see him anymore. She said she felt that he would never trust her, and that trust was what *she* thought love was all about. Paul felt bad, but he'd known it was coming all along, and he said to himself, "It's a good thing I never allowed myself to get jealous over someone as disloyal as Robin."

DIRECT-ATTACK
DAVE

Dave doesn't waste any time with subtle detective techniques. He feels that jealousy should be dealt with swiftly and harshly. That way, it can be eliminated before it becomes uncomfortable. Dave doesn't think about his jealousy, or talk about it—he just acts on it. Here's how he describes his approach:

"Last Saturday I took my girl to a party. Soon after we arrived, a big tall guy started talking to her. I didn't like him right from the start. He was one of those big-shot know-it-all types. He was talking to my girl for about twenty minutes. I could see him moving in. Finally I went up to him and told him to buzz off and find his own girl, because this one was with me. Well, he didn't like that very much! One thing led to another, and before long we were throwing punches. I gave it to him good! He deserved it, too.

"When I took my girl home, I told her what a weakling that guy was. Boy, was I surprised when she told me that she was embarrassed and angry that I had made a scene and spoiled the party! She told me she didn't want to see me for a while, until she could think things over. Well, I figure it this way—I may have gotten a few bruises, but at least I never got suckered into letting that know-it-all weakling turn me into a jealous chump!"

REVERSE-PSYCHOLOGY RITA

Rita would never admit to being jealous. Why should she? If she even suspects that a boy she's interested in is flirting with someone else, she just uses reverse psychology. Here's how Rita plays her game:

"Sure, I was a little bit concerned when I noticed that Stewart was hanging around Annie. But I never let on. That's really not the way to do things. You've got to let a boy know that he doesn't matter enough to get jealous about.

"I fixed myself up—I started running to take off a few extra pounds, and I tried to look as terrific as possible all the time. Whenever Stewart saw me, I made sure he saw that other boys were interested in me, too. I wanted Stewart to be so worried about losing *me* that he would forget all about Annie. Sure, this is game playing and it's dishonest, but so what? It's better than being a loser and letting someone know that he can make me jealous!"

BEN THE SELF-
BLAMER

When Ben feels jealous, he indulges in excessive doses of self-pity. Recently, for example, he saw his girlfriend, Francine, having lunch with Joel, the president of the science club. Ben felt all the elements of jealousy—anger, fear, rejection, and shame. But he denied his feelings completely. Instead, he sank into the nearest corner and blamed himself. Here's the kind of thing that went through his mind:

"I know Joel really has it all together. He's not only handsome, he's a real brain. If only I was smarter and better-looking, and had been more kind and loving to Francine! If I had paid more attention to her when I had the chance, she probably wouldn't be two-timing me now."

Ben sank so low into his own misery that he avoided Francine for the rest of the day. He didn't bother to call her that evening, as he usually did. He figured, "Why make it any harder for her? She obviously wants to get rid of me." And he thought, "Who can blame her? I'm not the kind of guy who can compare to someone like Joel. I'm not good enough for someone like Francine. Who was I kidding, anyway?"

The next day, Francine confronted Ben. She asked him why he hadn't called, and why he had been avoiding her. Ben was so afraid of admitting his jealous feelings that he claimed he didn't know what Francine was talking about. He assured her that nothing was wrong. But Ben continued to play his self-blaming game, and continued to avoid Francine. She felt rejected and hurt. She came to the logical conclusion that Ben no longer cared for her. She decided he must be interested in someone else. She had no idea how much Ben was hurting. You can see what a no-win situation Ben had put himself into by refusing to tell Francine his true feelings.

POSSESSIVE PAMELA

Pamela has developed a jealousy game that she's sure will always work. It's called Exclusive Ownership. When Pamela has difficulty dealing with her jealous feelings, she doesn't try to unravel them and share them with someone she trusts. Instead she makes her boyfriend, Ross, promise that he won't talk to other girls. At least that's what she made him promise at first. Now she also makes him promise not to go out with the boys, and not to be away from the phone when she calls. If Ross objects, Pamela threatens never to see him again.

Pamela believes that loving Ross means she

possesses him—exclusively. She also believes that dealing with her jealousy is Ross's responsibility. She figures that jealousy wouldn't be a problem if Ross didn't socialize with other girls (or go out with his friends, or stay after school for math club or track practice).

Pamela's positive that she's playing a winning game. It's worked so far, hasn't it? Well, no—it hasn't. Ross is tired of being owned, and he's just about ready to tell Pamela that her jealousy has gotten way out of hand. He feels suffocated and oppressed and he wants out of their relationship. Pamela may be too much of an expert at the jealousy game after all.

WHY GAMES DON'T WORK

The Private Eye, the Direct Attack, Reverse Psychology, Self-Blame, and Exclusive Ownership aren't the only jealousy games—you might know a few more yourself. The point is that, eventually, whoever plays these games loses. It's not difficult to figure out why: *denying jealousy and disguising it do not make it go away.* Jealousy games are just cosmetic—they only cover up problems, they don't cure them. Curing jealousy isn't impossible, but to begin treatment, you must first be honest with yourself.

SELF-HONESTY

Before you can begin to conquer the green-eyed monster, you must first admit that you have seen it. Paul, Dave, Rita, Ben, and Pamela never did that. If they had, they would have understood that jealousy games are silly, pointless, and potentially destructive.

How and when does self-honesty begin? It begins as soon as you think you are experiencing the first warning pangs of jealousy. Let's take it step by step. Suppose you see the person you love with someone else, and suppose you think that he might be interested in, or attracted to, that someone. What should you do?

STEP ONE—DO NOTHING! That's right. Don't take any immediate action. Remember, Dave believed in direct (and immediate) attack, and Rita believed in flirting to get even. Both those ploys backfired, and they were both dishonest.

At first, you'll need time to assess the situation and to think about what you're really feeling. If you act before you have a chance to do this, understanding your jealousy will be very difficult, and controlling it will be impossible.

STEP TWO—ASK YOURSELF THESE QUESTIONS:
   "What am I angry about?"
   "What am I afraid of?"

"Why do I feel rejected?"

"Why am I ashamed?"

Remember, jealousy is a combination of emotions. Isolating the different parts of jealousy will help you to figure out how they are interacting and why they are making you feel the way you do. It may take quite a while and a lot of soul-searching to answer these four questions. You might want to write about them, or you might want to talk about them with a friend. That's okay. But make sure you have answered these questions *honestly* before you go on to the next step.

STEP THREE—COMMUNICATE! After you've been honest with yourself and you know what you're feeling, you'll have to communicate your feelings to the other person. That's right—unlike Paul, Dave, Rita, Ben, and Pamela, you're going to depend on the truth, not on playing games.

Telling the truth means exposing parts of yourself—your fears and weaknesses. It also means admitting that you care a great deal about the other person. And when you come to think about it, isn't this what most jealousy games are really all about? Game players just can't bring themselves to say, "I need to know that you care about me as much as I care about you."

It's important to let the person you love know that you love him and that your jealous feelings are disturbing to you. After you've done this, you'll have to ask him for his help and understanding in dealing with the jealous feelings. You'll have to *share* your thoughts with him. Don't make the mistake of just *telling* him how silly, immature, or flirtatious you think he is. Remember, if you put someone down or attack him, he will only try to defend himself—and then your jealousy will be buried in a barrage of insults and accusations.

TIME-OUT

Whenever you find yourself on the brink of a jealousy game, call a time-out. Be honest with yourself and analyze the situation. Once you've done that, you'll have to break all the rules of all the jealousy games. That means playing it straight. Here's the difference between playing it straight and playing a game:

You're jealous and you feel *suspicious*.

PLAYING THE GAME: You follow the other person and call him constantly, hoping to catch him doing something to confirm your suspicions. When and if you do catch him, you confront him and let him fry!

PLAYING IT STRAIGHT: You talk to the person you love in the following way: "I tried to call you last night. My fantasy was that you were with someone else, someone you care about more than me." Don't accuse, don't blame, just talk about *your* feelings. Give your boyfriend time to think and to respond. If he seems uncomfortable, it's up to you to reassure him. And *listen* to what he has to say.

You're jealous and you feel *ready to attack* someone for flirting with the person you love.

PLAYING THE GAME: You punch the other person, or you cut her down with a few catty, well-chosen barbs. You feel superior—after all, you showed her just who's boss and who the real winner is!

PLAYING IT STRAIGHT: You hold back on your first impulse to strike out. You wait for a time when you can be alone with your boyfriend— preferably when you have cooled down enough to talk quietly and calmly. You explain: "She was paying a lot of attention to you. It made me feel threatened and uncomfortable." Don't make it seem that it was anyone's *fault.* Just talk about how the incident made *you* feel. Let your boyfriend know that you need to be assured that he cares about you, and give him an opportunity to express his feelings.

You're jealous and you feel like *using a bit of reverse psychology.*

PLAYING THE GAME: You take the attitude that it couldn't matter less to you what your boyfriend does. You switch on the charm at high power and make sure everyone knows that you're not jealous—just cool, unconcerned, and *very* attractive to members of the opposite sex.

PLAYING IT STRAIGHT: You admit you're jealous. You tell your boyfriend, "I felt jealous when I saw you with so-and-so. My first impulse was to flirt with someone else to make *you* jealous of *me*. But, I'd rather be honest with you and lay my cards on the table." You may be shaking as you say this, but you are on the right track!

You're jealous and you feel like *sinking into a sea of self-blame.*

PLAYING THE GAME: You automatically assume that your relationship is threatened by a third party. You withdraw. You assume that if things aren't going well, it's all your fault. You assume that the relationship is doomed, and you stop communicating with your partner entirely.

PLAYING IT STRAIGHT: You feel upset and afraid, but you take the other person aside and say, "I saw you with so-and-so" or "I heard that you were dating another person. It made me feel that I might have done something to make you unhappy. What does all this mean?" You don't sink into immediate self-pity or jump to gloomy conclusions. You give the other person a chance to clarify the situation.

You're jealous and you feel *possessive.*

PLAYING THE GAME: You lay down the law to your partner. You tell him that he can't eat lunch with or be friends with certain people.

You say that if he does, you'll never go out with him again.

PLAYING IT STRAIGHT: You explain: "I know we haven't made an agreement that we can't be friendly with other people, but when I saw you with so-and-so, I was surprised. I didn't expect it. I felt embarrassed." Wait for the other person to give you the details. Don't jump to conclusions. Discuss why you were embarrassed or upset. Ask if maybe you can both think of a way to deal with these incidents in the future.

GAMES YOU
SHOULDN'T PLAY

Jealousy games are different from other games. No one ever wins them, and they aren't even fun—so why play them?

Getting your jealousy under control isn't easy. No one ever said it was. But life becomes a lot more difficult when your jealousy begins to control *you*. The green-eyed monster *can* be tamed. It may rise up again every now and then. But if you have the right weapons, you can keep it under control. Honesty is the most powerful weapon you can use against jealousy. And honesty means being honest with *yourself*, as well as with the person you love.

If you're tormented by jealousy, try playing it straight for a while. Call a time-out to your particular jealousy game. If you really try to deal with your feelings directly, the odds are good that you and your partner will wind up with a real victory to celebrate!

Jealousy Quiz

Are you the jealous type? Are you playing a game in your love relationship—or are you playing it straight? Check the answer that best describes your reaction to each situation described below. You might be surprised by what this simple test indicates about your own "green-eyed monster."

1. You call the person you love late at night. He isn't in. You:
   A. Leave a message asking him to call back.
   B. Stay up all night worrying that he is with someone else.
   C. Call back a second time and use a phony voice just to make sure he really isn't at home. (After all, he might just be avoiding you.)
2. You're at a party with the person you love. He is talking with someone else. You:
   A. Notice it, but decide not to intrude.
   B. Sulk in a corner and think that you are losing him.
   C. Go right over there and break it up.

114

3. The person you care about wants to go to a game or a movie with his friends. You aren't invited. You:
   A. Say "Have a good time" and make other plans for that evening.
   B. Think that he just wants to get rid of you by going.
   C. Forbid him to go and threaten to break up if he does.
4. You hear a rumor that the person you love is dating someone else. You:
   A. Call him up and ask if it's true.
   B. Try to find out if it's true by asking all the people you know.
   C. Accept a date with someone else just to get even.
5. You notice that one of your friends is interested in the boy you love. You:
   A. Tell your boyfriend what you've noticed and talk about your feelings with him.
   B. Sink into a depression, sure your friend will steal your love away.
   C. Tell your friend she had better stay away from the person you love, or else!
6. The person you love decides to transfer to another school. You:
   A. Discuss how this will affect your relationship and try to think of ways you can arrange to see each other often.
   B. Say "Out of sight, out of mind," and try to forget him, since you're sure he'll forget you, too.

     C. Try to figure out ways to force him to stay at the same school with you, and hint that you may break up if he doesn't.
7. The boy you love seems interested in someone else. You:
     A. Decide to watch and wait. In the meantime, you don't push yourself on him, but you do let him know that you care.
     B. Give up and admit that you can't compete. In your mind, it's all over.
     C. Start to flirt with all of his close friends so he can see how much there is to lose by losing you.
8. The person you love gets a summer job where he will be around a lot of other girls. You:
     A. Talk over your worries and insecurity honestly, but try not to discourage him from taking the job—it's a good one.
     B. Sneak around the place where he's working and try to catch him with someone else.
     C. Try to get a job at the same place, or make friends with other people who work there so you can keep track of your boyfriend's every move.
9. Your boyfriend's parents ask him to take out a cousin who is visiting from out of town. You:
     A. Say "Okay, I understand." After all, they *are* cousins.
     B. Are afraid that your boyfriend isn't really telling you the truth—that it isn't really his cousin at all.

C. Say "Two can play at this game" and go out with someone else on the same night—making sure your boyfriend knows you are doing it.

10. The person you love joins the school track team. This means that you can see each other only on the weekends. You:

   A. Try to join a club or find an interest that will keep you busy during the week, too.

   B. Figure that joining the track team was his way of getting rid of you, and start looking for someone else. ½

   C. Say that since he is so busy you are going out with someone else—maybe even his close friend.

YOUR SCORE

Give yourself one point for every "A" answer, two points for every "B" answer, and three points for every "C" answer. Then add up your score.

10 points: Congratulations! You're not playing any games, and you're secure in your relationship. You know that being honest and straightforward is the best way to keep that special someone in your life.

11 to 20 points: Watch out! Your jealousy may be getting out of control. You need to feel better about yourself. You also need to have more open and honest talks with the person you love. You may be living with a lot of insecurity—and that can ruin your loving feelings.

20 to 30 points: You've got a green-eyed monster in your closet! You'd better read this chapter over a second time. Jealousy is getting the better of you, and nothing can be worse for your relationship.

CHAPTER NINE

Commitment

Most people think it means forever. Sometimes it does. But not always. Commitment can be a confusing word, because it means different things to different people at different times in their lives. No matter how old you are, or what kind of commitment you may be ready to make, you need to give the subject a lot of thought, because commitment isn't something you can undertake by yourself. It involves two people.

THE WAY IT USED
TO BE

A long time ago, no one ever had to think about commitments. That's because parents promised their children to their future husbands or wives at birth. They even set the date for the wedding, and if the children objected, they rarely had any choice or say in the matter. Today things are very different. You are able to make many of these decisions for yourself. And although that's probably a lot better than having them made for you, it's also a lot more difficult.

THE WAY IT IS NOW

Although your parents can't force you to make certain decisions, they *can* influence your choices. So can your friends. Before you make a commitment of any kind—whether it's to date someone on a regular basis, or to do something much more serious, like get engaged—it's a good idea to talk things over with people you trust. And, of course, you should talk things over with the person you love.

It may sound silly, but many people make commitments without ever talking it over with *anyone*. They find themselves in the position of assuming they have a special or exclusive arrangement with someone else, when they really don't. You don't want this to happen to you!

Formal agreements may be old-fashioned, but no agreement is foolish. If you are thinking of making some kind of commitment, you *must* talk it over with the person you love. If you don't, you won't know the limits and freedoms of your situation. You won't know what to expect, or what is expected of you.

DON'T DEPEND ON ESP

The first rule in making commitments is: don't assume that the person you love loves you in return, and is ready to make a commitment, until he says so. And don't assume that the kind of arrangement you have in mind is the same kind *he* has in mind. Mind-reading and ESP may work in some situations, but they never work when it comes to commitments. You may *think* you know just what he's thinking, and you may even be right—but how can you be sure? Certainly not by gazing into a crystal ball—or by hoping. The only way you can know for sure is to ask. And the only way you can know for sure that you have an agreement is to talk about it and actually say, "Yes, now we have an agreement."

THE RULES OF
THE GAME

Can you imagine what it would be like if you tried to play baseball without knowing the rules of the game—without knowing what had been decided and agreed upon beforehand? It would be pretty difficult to accomplish your goals; in fact, nothing would make any sense at all. After a while you'd probably become frustrated and give up completely. It works exactly the same way in a relationship. The rules—boundaries, responsibilities, rights, and freedoms—must be discussed and agreed upon in advance if you want things to work. And that's what commitment is really all about. *It's an agreement between two people about the kind of relationship they both want.*

KNOW YOURSELF

How will you feel if the boy you love makes friends with other girls? Participates in activities that don't include you? Travels without you? Occasionally dates someone else? These are just some of the questions that you'll need to think about before you can make a commitment. In order to answer them honestly, you will have to do some soul-searching. Once you've done that, you will know yourself a little bit better; you'll have some idea of what you expect and need in a relationship. The next step is to share that knowledge with the person you love.

A commitment, whether it is informal or serious, is always an agreement between two selves—your self, and the self of the person you love. This means you have to consider what *you* want and what will be comfortable for *you*, but it also means you have to consider someone else's comfort and someone else's self. Sometimes what you want and need, and what you can tolerate, can be different from what your boyfriend wants, needs, and can tolerate. That's when it becomes necessary to talk and to negotiate.

THE BALANCE SHEET

Once you begin to talk and negotiate the type of commitment you want, you may find that the person you love has different feelings about different issues. This doesn't mean that you aren't really in love, or that he doesn't care for you. It just means that the two of you are different in some ways. When you've got *that* figured out, you really start to get down to the nitty-gritty of making a commitment.

You probably feel there are some things you want to insist upon; you might not feel so strongly about others. Your boyfriend will also want to insist upon certain things. Each of you may have to make sacrifices and compromises to reach a satisfactory agreement. Before you make a final commitment, draw up a mental balance sheet, and as you look it over, ask yourself these important questions:

"Are the sacrifices I'm being asked to make reasonable, or do they overstep some important personal boundaries?"

"Is he giving up some of his demands to meet me halfway?"

"Is this a balanced relationship, or is one of us giving in to the other?"

"Is this an arrangement I can really live with? Does it go against any of my values and beliefs, or any needs I consider just too important to give up?"

"Can I honestly live up to what he expects of me? Can he honestly live up to my expectations?"

"Are we using words like 'forever,' 'never,' and 'always' realistically, or are we just saying them to please and to comfort each other?"

"Is it possible to delay this decision until we can come up with a more equally balanced (and more realistic) commitment?"

WHEN IS THE RIGHT TIME TO MAKE A COMMITMENT?

There are many different kinds of commitments, and there is no one right time for making any one of them. But there *are* wrong times. One wrong time is before you know someone well, or before you trust him. Another wrong time is before you've had an opportunity to discuss the nature of your agreement thoroughly, to think about it, perhaps to discuss it with someone you trust (like your parents or a good friend). It's also the wrong time to make a commitment if you are confused, worried, or upset about other people or other events in your life.

The right time to make a commitment is when you are involved with someone you care about, and both of you agree that it's time to get closer and deepen the relationship. This doesn't mean that you will both feel exactly the same way at exactly the same time. More likely one partner will feel it first, and will have to tell the other just what he or she is experiencing.

It can be exciting to feel that you want to make a commitment to another person. It can be so exciting that you don't manage to communicate your feelings to the other person clearly. If this happens, you might begin to feel that you are in a relationship with someone you really care about, but that things are just not working out the way you'd like them to. If you think about it, the reason for this isn't very strange. When the terms of a relationship are not clearly discussed and agreed upon, there is bound to be some uneasiness and insecurity. You may think that your relationship means one thing, and your partner may think that it means something entirely different. That's when it's time to sit down and talk about what you'd *both* like it to mean. And once you reach an agreement, that's the right time to begin making a commitment!

CHAPTER TEN

Breaking Up

Breaking up really is hard to do. It's especially difficult when someone breaks up with you. Sometimes two people break up because they both agree that things just can't be worked out. But many times, breaking up occurs when one person decides he or she wants to end the relationship. And that means the other person can be left with some broken dreams—and even a broken heart. Just how do you cope if you happen to be that other person?

DON'T BLAME
YOURSELF

Sure, you might have made some mistakes; you might even have hurt the person you loved. But don't take *all* the blame. Blaming yourself can cause you to draw some pretty depressing conclusions—conclusions like:

"I'm just too selfish, to dishonest, or too jealous to have a successful relationship."

"No one will ever love me again."

"I made a mess of this, and I'll probably do the same thing next time. I'd better forget all about love . . . forever."

Taking all the blame can also prevent you from understanding what went wrong, and how you can change things the next time. And it can make you forget one very important point: it takes *two* to make or break a relationship.

Too much self-blame can lead to self-pity. Feeling sorry for yourself for an extended period of time is likely to isolate you from your friends, your family, and even from someone new who might be waiting to meet you. And self-pity can do something else—it can cause you to conclude that you are unlovable. When you feel unlovable, you don't like yourself. These are troubling feelings, and, after a while, they can undermine your security and your self-confidence. So it's important to learn how to cope with breaking up without letting it break your spirit.

GOOD ADVICE
THAT DOESN'T
WORK

Well-meaning friends and family members might tell you that breaking up is something you'll forget about in a few weeks. They might say, "You'll probably laugh at this tomorrow." Or they might tell you that breaking up is part of growing up, and that you're better off without him. All of these things may be true. But you probably won't believe any of them when you hear them. That's because breaking up is always painful—no matter how old you are, or how serious your relationship was. While you're feeling it, the pain is very real. Sometimes it seems as if *no one* understands what you're going through. When you feel that way, the world becomes a hostile place.

Your feelings of pain and sadness are natural. You don't have to deny them, and you don't have to pretend that there's nothing wrong. Sometimes being honest and saying, "I feel hurt and disappointed, and I guess I will feel this way for a while," will help your friends and your family to understand that you can't always be talked or joked out of your blue moods.

Rx FOR A BROKEN
HEART

What will help you recover? The best medicine for a broken heart is time. But time can move very slowly. Some days you may feel that you'll never be happy again. But there are a few things you can do to lighten your misery. Try a few of these remedies. . . .

DO SOMETHING NICE FOR YOURSELF. That's right—go to a movie; buy yourself something you've been wanting for a while; take a walk, a hike, a long hot bath; enjoy your favorite meal; go swimming; spend some time in a place you love, with people you love. Doing something nice for yourself helps you to feel that you *do* count. Pampering yourself is a way to remind yourself that you *are* lovable, after all.

DON'T MAKE YOURSELF MISERABLE. You're probably miserable enough. Don't add to your blue feelings by going places where the two of you went together, or by looking over old photographs, letters, or mementoes. There will be a time when these things won't make you upset, but that time is not now. And don't try to get in touch with or talk to the boy you just broke up with until you have gotten through this rough period. Don't attempt to relive memories that are still bittersweet.

DON'T LOOK FOR AN IMMEDIATE REPLACEMENT. After breaking up, some people think they'll never fall in love again. But others feel that they *must* fall in love again—immediately! Trying to find a new love right away really isn't a very good idea. Rushing from one relationship into another won't allow you the time you need to recover, and to analyze what went wrong. The hurt won't disappear if you invest all your energies in a new relationship; you'll only be covering up some very important and normal feelings. Rushing into a new relationship has another drawback— it can prevent you from using your best judgment. You might mistake need for love. In other words, in your haste, you might choose someone who isn't really right for you. Wait a while before you begin to see someone steadily. Dating is fine, but you need and *deserve* some breathing room right now.

GET A LITTLE HELP FROM YOUR FRIENDS. Although this may not be the time for a new love, it *is* the time for old (good, and trusted) friends. Call them. Get together. Do some of the things you always enjoyed doing with friends. Joining a club or a team or getting involved with new activities helps, too. Keeping busy with interesting activities not only helps you to feel good about yourself, it helps the time pass more quickly.

TAKE ON A NEW CHALLENGE. Is there something you've always wanted to do—something that isn't easy, that's challenging and requires an investment of time and energy? Something like learning to play an instrument, speak a foreign language, master a sport? Or like getting in shape, building something, making the honor roll? Just about everyone can think of something she's always wanted to do, but couldn't because she just didn't have the time or the energy. Well, now is the perfect time for you to take on that challenge. It will give you something really interesting to do. It will give you an alternative to sitting at home, staring out the window, watching TV, overeating, reliving events of the past. Most important, it will give you back something you might have temporarily lost—your self-confidence.

PUT THE ANGER BEHIND YOU. After breaking up with someone you love, you might blame yourself—you might think that it was all your fault. But there's another possibility—you might blame the other person. You might feel bitter and angry. You might even think about revenge.

It's natural to be hurt and even angry if you have been rejected, but it isn't natural (or good for you) to hold on to that anger, and to plan ways to "get even" or "show up" your former love. When you come to think of it, staying angry at someone is really a way to stay tied to him. Feelings of anger and even hatred may be different from feelings of love, but what remains the same is that much of your time is occupied with thoughts and dreams of someone who should be part of your past—not your present. Let the anger go. Don't dwell on how badly you might have been treated. Instead, think of how much you have to look forward to, how many new and different activities you have planned for the coming weeks and months. Don't let anger and revenge keep you locked in a relationship that is clearly over.

ALLOW YOURSELF SOME LAUGHTER. Laughing may seem like the last thing you want to do right now—but it's terrific medicine. Whenever you begin to think sad thoughts about your former love, substitute a different picture in your mind. Picture him doing something funny—something ridiculous. Visualize him wearing a silly costume, or saying or doing something completely out of character. This little mind game will help you to stop thinking about that someone quite so much, and it will help you to avoid becoming melancholy and morose. Most of all, it just might get you to smile instead of cry.

BEING FRIENDS

After you lose someone you love, you might discover that you've also lost your best friend. This can make breaking up more painful. To ease the pain, you might find yourself asking the person you loved:

"Can't we still be friends?"

Sometimes people who were once in love can be friends. Sometimes they can't. But for most people, it's best to wait a while. How long you wait depends upon how long it takes you to accept the fact that you really have broken up. You might want to be friends with someone you once loved because you enjoy his company and value his friendship. On the other hand, you might want to be friends because you still love him and are hoping that maybe, just maybe, if you remain friendly, your relationship will eventually turn into something deeper. Hopes like this are natural. But they are also attempts to deny the truth, and they can make accepting reality that much more difficult. What's more, forming a friendship with someone you still love can be unfair to him. If you aren't honest about your true feelings, if you use his friendship to avoid the pain that breaking up caused, then you won't really have much of a "friendship" at all. That's bad for you, and if will be bad for him, too. You and your former love should only try to be friends if you can build the relationship on good memories, affection, and—most of all—honesty.

WHAT'S NEXT

After some time has passed, you should be feeling like your old self again. Maybe you still have some unhappy moments, some times of sadness. Maybe you still miss that special person, and it still hurts when you see him or recall a precious memory. But once the hurt has begun to ease, and you have come to terms with the past and have put it behind you, you're ready for something else—starting over.

CHAPTER ELEVEN

Starting Over

*H*ere it comes again. That wonderful jittery feeling, that thrill when he smiles at you, that hope that he'll be home when you call. Whether it's love or just a strong attraction, you know one thing for sure—you're starting over.

A new relationship brings with it new hopes, new expectations, new happiness. The best thing about falling in love again is the rush of exciting feelings, the hopefulness, the sharing. Unfortunately, a new love relationship can also bring up some old worries. If you've had a disappointing experience with love, you may be worried that the same thing is going to happen to you again.

It's always wise to try to learn from your past mistakes. And if you've waited and allowed some time to pass before beginning a new relationship, you probably *have* learned something. You've probably thought about your last relationship, why it didn't work out, why you broke up. Maybe this time you plan to look for different qualities in a boy. Maybe you think that this time you'll want to make different kinds of commitments. Even if you do all this, you might still be asking yourself, "What if I get hurt again?"

TAKE IT ONE STEP AT A TIME

It seems pretty silly to think about how a relationship might end before it's even begun. But that's the way most people *do* think. Breaking up can be so upsetting that it can cause you to worry and to be overly cautious about new relationships. In a way this can be helpful. Being cautious means taking things one step at a time—slowly and thoughtfully. It means talking openly and honestly with your new boyfriend about all your feelings and fears. But being cautious doesn't mean being afraid to trust. It doesn't mean being so suspicious, so guarded, and so reluctant to share your self that you wind up alone.

Sharing is really what love is all about. And

that means sharing your thoughts and hopes, as well as all those little worries and nagging doubts. It might also mean sharing your fears and your concerns about the past. No one can guarantee that this time things will be completely different, but you can be pretty sure that if you keep the lines of communication open, they will be a lot better.

LEARN FROM
THE PAST

Once you've recovered from the disappointment of breaking up—look at your past and learn from it. If you think about your relationship and review it in your mind, you may discover some mistakes, some problems, and some misconceptions on your part that led to the breakup. If you reread the beginning of this book you might just discover that you and your boyfriend were in a love trap or were playing jealousy games. You might have been haunted by love ghosts, or you might have been unable to draw important boundaries around yourselves. No one can promise you that you won't make the same mistake twice, but if you learn more about yourself, and more about love, it's a good bet that your next relationship will be more successful.

CHAPTER TWELVE

Does True Love Last Forever?

*L*ots of people fall in love—they even get married. But when things don't work out, they break up or get divorced. This may seem confusing. It may cause you to wonder and even to worry. If you've ever been in love and been disappointed, you may feel skeptical; you might think that love can't possibly last. You might find yourself asking the big question: "Does true love last forever?"

It really *is* a big question, because it's something everyone asks at one time or another. But the answer isn't big or complicated at all. *Love will last forever if you know how to make it last that long.*

Wanting love to last forever, wishing for it, is just not enough. You've got to learn how to make it happen. You might want your favorite sweater to last for more than one or two seasons, but if you don't learn proper upkeep and you don't take good care of it, chances are it won't last nearly that long. Love involves upkeep and know-how, too. It involves checking up on your feelings and your partner's feelings. It may also involve repairing damage and wear and tear.

Love *can last forever.* It can also last for a week, or a year, or as long as you want it to. Love isn't something outside yourself, something over which you have no control. Love is a mixture of two people's needs, expectations, and emotions. It's a combination of your self and someone else's self. If you allow the mixture to become stale, or polluted, or weak, then it won't last. But if you take care of it, shake it up when it needs to be shaken, and give it lots of attention, then you'll have it—forever.

Your Love I.Q.

How much do you know about love? Are you haunted by love ghosts, troubled by jealousy, unable to draw boundaries, not ready to make a commitment? This quiz is designed to measure your love I.Q. It will help you discover just how much you know about love—and how much you need to learn.

Check the answer that best describes your reaction to each situation.

1. Someone you like very much, and might even love, is pursuing you. He wants a commitment. You're not sure you're ready to date just one person. You:

    A. Think it's better not to get too involved with anyone, because when you fall in love your whole life changes—maybe for the worse.

    B. Tell him you need some time to think things over, and then discuss your feelings with your friends and try to get a clearer perspective.

    C. Decide to plunge in and go steady. After

all, who knows if someone will ever fall in love with you again?

2. You've been dating someone for a while. You're pretty sure you're in love. You:
   A. Assume that the person you love must be having these same feelings and decide it's time for a serious commitment.
   B. Think about ending it now, before you become dependent and weak. After all, you could wind up with a broken heart.
   C. Decide to take a risk and tell him how you feel, and find out if he feels the same way.

3. You've gone out on a date with someone you really care about, but you haven't heard from him since. You:
   A. Call him up and ask him to go with you to a basketball game, movie, or other informal place.
   B. Assume that he was turned off by one of your many faults.
   C. Decide to go out with other people to make him notice you and want to ask you out again.

4. Someone you care about tells you he loves you. You:
   A. Figure he's just trying to get something out of you.
   B. Decide to talk about how *you* really feel, even if it might disappoint him.
   C. Become very uncomfortable and make a big joke out of it.

5. You've been dating someone for a long time. Things are getting boring, but no one's said anything yet. You:
   A. Break up. It's best to reject the other person before he rejects you.
   B. Buy him a gift or surprise him with a new hairdo or a new outfit, just to spice things up.
   C. Invite him over some afternoon for a private conversation and tell him what you've been thinking and what you're afraid of.

6. The person you love has some annoying habits that are getting to you. You:
   A. Decide what habits you can live with and which ones are really bugging you, and then talk it out with your boyfriend.
   B. Think that if you really love him you should be able to accept everything about him.
   C. Decide that if you accept these bad habits you'll become weak, a doormat who has to take bad treatment all the time.

7. Your best friend has two tickets to a rock concert. She invites you. You want to go, but the person you love can't because there are only two tickets. You:
   A. Say yes because you've got to look out for Number One.
   B. Say no because it wouldn't be fair to

leave out this special person—not if you really loved him.

    C. Say yes after you've explained the situation to your boyfriend, explaining that you'll miss him, but that this is one opportunity you don't want to pass up.

8. The person you love tells you he cares about you but wants to date other people. You:

    A. Decide not to put up with this rejection and tell him you never want to see him again.

    B. Say "Good, so do I" even though you don't really mean it and hope he will change his mind.

    C. Tell him you feel bad and you'll need time to decide whether this is an arrangement you can live with.

9. The person you love wants to borrow something of yours that you don't like to lend (your guitar, your radio, a book, or whatever). You:

    A. Gently explain that you aren't going to lend it to him because it is something you feel special about, something that is definitely "yours" and not "ours."

    B. Lend it to him because you feel it would be selfish not to.

    C. Say no without explaining. You figure he was just trying to use you, anyway.

10. You think you're in a love trap. You:

    A. Try to get the person you love to change his behavior.

B. Decide that you had both better examine your actions, and that probably you both need to make some changes.

C. Break up fast before you get trapped for life!

YOUR SCORE

Give yourself one, two, or three points for each of your answers, going by the list below. (For example: if you answered "A" on question 1, give yourself one point; but if you answered "B" give yourself three points, and if you answered "C" give yourself two points.)

Question 1: A = 1 point   B = 3 points C = 2 points
Question 2: A = 2 points B = 1 point   C = 3 points
Question 3: A = 3 points B = 1 point   C = 2 points
Question 4: A = 1 point   B = 3 points C = 2 points
Question 5: A = 1 point   B = 2 points C = 3 points
Question 6: A = 3 points B = 2 points C = 1 point
Question 7: A = 1 point   B = 2 points C = 3 points
Question 8: A = 1 point   B = 2 points C = 3 points
Question 9: A = 3 points B = 2 points C = 1 point
Question 10: A = 2 points B = 3 points C = 1 point

30 to 28 points: You're pretty smart. You've learned a lot about love and you know when, where, and to whom to express your feelings. Keep it up—you're learning more every day!

27 to 22 points: You have some of the right ideas, but you need to think more about what love ghosts may be haunting you, why you play jealousy games, and when it's best to draw boundaries.

21 to 10 points: Uh-oh. You're haunted by love ghosts that keep you from trusting yourself and others. You may want to read *The Sweet Dreams Love Book* over again and discuss the ideas in it with someone you trust.

ABOUT THE AUTHORS

DEIDRE S. LAIKEN, Ms. Ed., was born in New York and received her master's degree from the State University College at Buffalo. She was a classroom teacher for four years. Currently she is a full-time writer and the author of five books, including "Daughters of Divorce" (Morrow, 1981).

ALAN J. SCHNEIDER, M.S.W., C.S.W., is a practicing psychotherapist in Manhattan and New Jersey. He is a doctoral candidate at Columbia University.

Deidre Laiken and Alan Schneider are a husband-and-wife team who have written "Listen to Me, I'm Angry" (Lothrop, Lee & Shepard, 1980), which was named one of the best-written books of the year by the American Library Association. They divide their time between their apartment in metropolitan New York and their home in the Catskill Mountains.